Nelly Schuster

Coordinating Service Compositions

Model and Infrastructure for Collaborative Creation of Electronic Documents

Coordinating Service Compositions

Model and Infrastructure for Collaborative
Creation of Electronic Documents

by
Nelly Schuster

Dissertation, Karlsruher Institut für Technologie (KIT)
Fakultät für Wirtschaftswissenschaften
Tag der mündlichen Prüfung: 30. April 2013
Referenten: Prof. Dr. Stefan Tai, Prof. Dr. Schahram Dustdar

Impressum

Karlsruher Institut für Technologie (KIT)
KIT Scientific Publishing
Straße am Forum 2
D-76131 Karlsruhe
www.ksp.kit.edu

KIT – Universität des Landes Baden-Württemberg und
nationales Forschungszentrum in der Helmholtz-Gemeinschaft

KIT Scientific Publishing 2013
Print on Demand

ISBN 978-3-7315-0034-6

Coordinating Service Compositions
Model and Infrastructure for Collaborative
Creation of Electronic Documents

Zur Erlangung des akademischen Grades eines
Doktors der Ingenieurwissenschaften
(Dr.-Ing.)
von der Fakultät für
Wirtschaftswissenschaften
des Karlsruher Institut für Technologie (KIT)
genehmigte
DISSERTATION
von

Dipl.-Ing. (FH) Nelly Angelina Schuster

Tag der mündlichen Prüfung: 30. April 2013
Referent: Prof. Dr. Stefan Tai
Korreferent: Prof. Dr. Schahram Dustdar
Karlsruhe, Mai 2013

Abstract

Collaborative document creation enables humans to solve complex problems in a team, to exchange ideas, and to benefit from synergistic effects. Besides creating content, participants often gather contents from different sources. The Web, for instance, offers configurable and ever-changing data (e.g., multimedia contents, sensor data, maps) and services (e.g., for graphical transformations, calculations) which can perform activities during collaborative document creation. The *composition* of human contributions with data and services on the Web into a document, however, involves high manual effort of participants.

Dependencies between activities and content need to be *coordinated* (e.g., through division of labor, notifications, flow control), in order to avoid inconsistencies and additional effort and, hence, to increase quality of collaboration. Coordination, however, is complicated as often activities, participants, and required contents can not be defined completely in advance.

Tools for collaborative document creation, e.g., Web-based editors, do not support integration of contributions from the Web. Service oriented systems enable the integration of contributions of heterogeneous participants, however, focus on coordination of activities in structured and repeatable processes.

This thesis therefore introduces a novel model which maps contributions in collaborative document creation on a *service-oriented component model*. Services might represent contributions of humans; services, however, might also be an open number of software services on the Web. The composition model on top of the component model enables participants to flexibly compose these services into a document. Based on the evolving service composition, various coordination mechanisms can be applied which consider different requirements of collaborative document creation.

In order to illustrate feasibility of this novel form of collaborative document creation, a Web-based collaboration system was developed. In addition, two use cases were examined which expose different requirements as regards document model, participants, communication, and coordination. The realization of the use cases are enabled through configuration and extension points of the model. Thanks to its adaptability, the model can serve as framework and starting point for the development of innovative tools which support different scenarios of collaborative document creation through coordinated service compositions.

Zusammenfassung

Die gemeinsame Erstellung von Dokumenten ermöglicht das Erarbeiten komplexer Sachverhalte im Team, den Austausch von Ideen und das Nutzen von Synergieeffekten. Neben der Entwicklung von Inhalten tragen Beteiligte häufig Inhalte aus unterschiedlichen Quellen zusammen. Hierfür stellt beispielsweise das Web konfigurierbare oder sich ständig ändernde Daten bereit (z.B. Multimedia-Inhalte, Sensordaten, Karten) sowie eine große Anzahl an Diensten (z.B. zur grafischen Transformation, Berechnung), die Aufgaben während der gemeinsamen Dokumentenerstellung erfüllen können. *Komposition* von menschlichen Beiträgen mit Daten und Diensten aus dem Web in ein Dokument ist jedoch mit hohem manuellem Aufwand der Beteiligten verbunden. Abhängigkeiten von Aktivitäten und Inhalten im Dokument müssen *koordiniert* werden (z.B. durch Arbeitsteilung, Benachrichtigungen, Ablaufsteuerung), um z.B. Inkonsistenzen und Mehraufwand zu vermeiden und somit die Qualität der Zusammenarbeit zu verbessern. Die Koordination wird dadurch erschwert, dass häufig vorab nicht bestimmbar ist, wer wann welche Beiträge erbringt.

Werkzeuge zur gemeinsamen Dokumentenerstellung, z.B. Web-basierte Editoren, unterstützen keine Integration von Beiträgen aus dem Web. Dienstorientierte Systeme ermöglichen zwar die Integration unterschiedlicher Beteiligter, erlauben aber insbesondere die Koordination von Aktivitäten in strukturierten, planbaren und wiederholbaren Prozessen.

Diese Arbeit stellt deshalb ein neuartiges Modell vor, das Beiträge zur gemeinsamen Dokumentenerstellung auf ein *dienstorientiertes Komponentenmodell* abbildet. Bei Diensten kann es sich hierbei sowohl um von Menschen erbrachte Leistungen handeln als auch um eine offene Anzahl von Softwarediensten im Web. Das auf dem Komponentenmodell aufbauende Kompositionsmodell ermöglicht es den Beteiligten, diese Dienste flexibel in ein Dokument zusammenzusetzen. Basierend auf der sich entwickelnden Dienstkomposition können verschiedene Koordinationsmechanismen angewandt werden, die spezifische Anforderungen der gemeinsamen Dokumentenerstellung berücksichtigen.

Um die Umsetzbarkeit dieser neuartigen Form der gemeinsamen Dokumentenerstellung zu illustrieren, wurden ein Web-basiertes Kollaborationssystem implementiert sowie zwei Anwendungsfälle untersucht, die unterschiedliche Anforderungen bezüglich Dokumentenmodell, Beteiligten, Kommunikation und Koordination aufweisen. Die Realisierung der Anwendungsfälle wurde durch die Konfigurierbarkeit und Erweiterbarkeit des Modells ermöglicht. Dank dieser Anpassbarkeit kann das Modell als Rahmenwerk und Ausgangspunkt dienen zur Entwicklung innovativer Werkzeuge, die verschiedenartige Szenarien der gemeinsamen Dokumentenerstellung durch koordinierte Dienstkomposition unterstützen.

Danksagung

Wie die meisten anderen Dissertationen, ist auch meine nicht in alleiniger Arbeit im stillen Kämmerchen entstanden. Deshalb möchte ich meinen Wegbegleitern zum Doktorgrad herzlichen Dank aussprechen.

Ich danke Prof. Dr. Stefan Tai für die engagierte Betreuung durch ausführliche Rückmeldungen, hilfreiche Anregungen und Diskussionen, die vorbehaltlose Unterstützung inhaltlicher und organisatorischer Art und das stete Interesse an der Thematik der Arbeit. Stefan und das Team Ökonomie und Technologie der eOrganisation (eOrg) des Karlsruher Instituts für Technologie (KIT) haben dafür gesorgt, dass die Dissertationszeit sehr kurzweilig war und angenehm verlief.

Ich danke Prof. Dr. Schahram Dustdar für seinen freundlichen Einsatz als Korreferent sowie Prof. Dr. Andreas Oberweis und Prof. Dr. Karl-Heinz Waldmann, die das Prüfungskomitee vervollständigten.

Ich danke Dr. Christian Zirpins für die wertvolle inhaltliche und wissenschaftliche Begleitung und das hilfreiche Feedback zur schriftlichen Ausarbeitung.

Ich danke allen momentanen und ehemaligen Mitgliedern des eOrg-Teams für die zahlreichen Diskussionen und kritischen Anmerkungen zu Inhalt und Präsentation der Dissertation, für die unkomplizierte Zusammenarbeit und sehr gute Teamatmosphäre. Ich danke meinen Mitautoren Dr. Ulrich Scholten (DYNO-Pattern-Repository), Erik Wittern und Jörn Kuhlenkamp (kollaborative Service-Feature-Modellierung) sowie Raffael Stein und Studenten (Demonstratoren). Es freut mich besonders, von Beginn an dabei gewesen zu sein und das Team wachsen gesehen zu haben.

Ich danke Prof. Dr. Jens Nimis und den Kollegen vom FZI Forschungszentrum Informatik und Karlsruhe Service Research Institute (KSRI) für Feedback und Inspiration in frühen Phasen der Arbeit, sowie Rita Schmidt und Heike Döhmer für die großartige administrative Unterstützung.

Ich danke meinem Diplomarbeitsbetreuer am IBM Forschungslabor in Zürich, Prof. Dr. Olaf Zimmermann, mich darin bestärkt zu haben, dieses Vorhaben anzugehen, und die Einführung in's wissenschaftliche Arbeiten.

Ich danke dem Karlsruhe House of Young Scientists (KHYS) für die Unterstützung des kurzen Forschungsaufenthalts bei HP Labs in Palo Alto durch ein Stipendium.

Ich danke allen, die während der Arbeit, auf Konferenzen oder durch anonyme Reviews von Publikationen Gedankenanstöße und Anregungen für diese Arbeit gegeben haben.

Ich danke meiner Familie und guten Freunden, die das Leben lebenswert machen.

Nelly Schuster

Contents

Part I.

Foundations

1. Introduction

1.1. Motivation and Problem Statement

Human collaboration is crucial for creative and knowledge intense activities. For example, scientists collaboratively author research publications or project proposals, software engineers jointly model and code large systems, or IT management staff capture and discuss incidents. Such collaborations often are situational, weakly structured, and highly interactive. Further, *documents* play a critical role in such collaboration. On the one hand, individuals communicate and coordinate with each other in order to reach a common goal, which is manifested in an evolving but coherent document. On the other hand, documents provide a means of communicating and sharing information [83] in a purpose-optimized, e.g., structured, annotated, graphically appealing, legally binding form of representation in order to share and clarify individual points-of-view and dispute with targeted recipients [136].

A large range of *collaborative document creation* processes exist during which manifold electronic documents are created. These processes include collaborative writing, modeling, knowledge management, and software documentation. To give an example, a project proposal is a non-trivial document where several organizations contribute distinct parts of the proposal document (e.g., an overview picture of the planned solution, a text describing the contributions of the organization to the project) or perform specific activities like proofreading or publishing the document. Figure 1.1 shows an example project proposal during development.

Such collaborations are characterized by the incremental evolution of content through interrelated activities including ad hoc changes. In the beginning of the collaboration its activities and their exact order are not known, and therefore, equally the required knowledge and skills as well as who participates at which point in time are unknown. Activities might be the provisioning of new knowledge and data as well as the transformation (e.g., translation or proofread) or publication of existing data. Activities are performed in a situational manner, for instance, new subtasks might be identified during discussions among project partners. Thus, not all document parts and activities can be explicitly modeled but may simply appear during process execution.

In order to reach the goal, activities need to be *coordinated*. Coordination includes automated detection and avoidance of potential inconsistencies of shared resources (e.g., a section in the document is edited by several authors) and the support of temporal dependencies (e.g.,

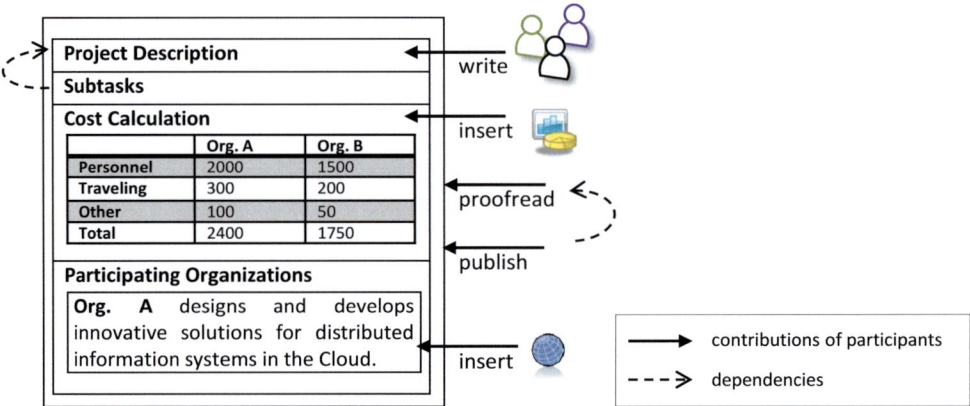

Figure 1.1.: Project proposal writing as example of collaborative document creation.

a diagram of data can only be created after the data has been delivered, or the document can only be published if it is proofread). For example, in the Information Technology Infrastructure Library (ITIL) [79] a number of key processes for IT service providers are described like incident and problem management. The processes require situational collaborations between employees of the service providers, their clients, and possibly external experts. For the management of knowledge bases, e.g., software pattern repositories, participants often need to agree on a common structure of the patterns. The size of the group as well as a process, however, are not prescribed. Accordingly, collaboration processes include a mixture of well-structured parts which are known in advance and flexible and unexpected aspects [13]. Coordination mechanisms need to support this continuum.

Contents and data used and created throughout the collaboration might stem from different sources. Sources might be humans, enterprise systems, or other documents, available in manifold formats and structures. More and more services are offered on the Web providing content or information which can be used in collaboration. Modern documents include interactive contents like video, social media, or maps. Moreover, a lot of services exist which solve problems or perform simple tasks for humans, e.g., language translators, layout or publishing services, or sensors. Using these services throughout the collaboration means that activities are also performed by non-human participants. The integration of such content and services is challenging, since they expose different data formats and interfaces. Such content and services might change unexpectedly and uncontrolled by the human participants of a collaboration. In the project proposal example mentioned above, data is included from different sources, for instance, the project description paragraph and subtasks are written by different persons, tables for cost calculation stem from a software system, and the description of the organization is extracted from the Web. The Web also offers a large number of services and tools for humans to collaborate, communicate, or share and collaboratively manage information, e.g., collaborative real time editors, chat applications, file shares, or social networks. As a result, collaboration is performed, content delivered, and information exchanged through various, often disconnected information channels. This might cause a loss of information [89] or communication overhead.

Process-driven models and tools address coordination requirements of processes performed by different participants. Using these solutions, participants model in advance who is allowed to contribute what at which part of the document at which time. Process-driven solutions coordinate the collaboration and increase efficiency. These approaches support highly structured and routine processes, e.g., through workflow management systems. The solutions do not allow for unplanned changes which are required especially in creative kinds of collaboration. Various approaches strive to support flexible coordination of collaborative processes (cf. [22][26][38][145]). These solutions, however, most often regard repeatable business processes and do not consider documents.

The Web facilitates more flexible forms of collaboration and information consolidation. A multitude of Web-based text processing and collaboration services facilitate cooperation of geographically dispersed authors, e.g., Zoho[1] or Google Docs[2]. Such services allow participants to contribute anytime in any part of the document and enable flexibility regarding ad hoc contributions and document structure. None of the quoted solutions, however, explicitly supports coordination of activities. Most often, specific types of documents are supported, e.g., text or spreadsheets. The integration of non-human participants into collaboration, however, is not enabled.

As regards integration of content, services, and communication channels into documents, service-oriented computing (SOC) technologies are promising as they allow for the integration and composition of more flexible process-driven information systems and for mashing up situational end-user applications [153][131]. SOC suits to integrate and compose heterogeneous services as reusable functional entities from different sources. SOC simplifies ubiquitous access and provides the ability to flexibly scale as regards users and produced data. A number of solutions for the integration of humans into service-oriented applications exist (e.g., [120][99]). Available service composition models, however, offer coordination means which are too rigid in order to support human collaboration. Service mashups enable the end-user driven composition and integration of dynamic contents. Mashup approaches, however, do not consider the collaborative creation of documents.

To summarize, collaboration on and mediated through documents comprises a range of unstructured to structured human-driven processes. Solutions to support such collaborations need to balance flexibility and coordination. Although SOC offers promising technologies

---

[1] http://docs.zoho.com/ (accessed January 2nd, 2013)
[2] http://docs.google.com/ (accessed January 2nd, 2013)

for the flexible integration and composition of heterogeneous content into different types of documents, service composition is not leveraged for collaborative document creation.

1.2. Research Hypothesis and Contributions

The hypothesis underlying this thesis is that the mapping of the case of collaborative document creation on a service component and composition model facilitates (a) the integration and composition of contributions provided by humans and software systems in such collaborations and (b) the coordination of such collaborations through mechanisms adapted to the needs of the participants. The main idea is to represent documents as *compositions of services*. Content provisioning, transformation, or publishing activities are mapped to services delivering contents which can be composed into documents. Services are delivered by humans or other kinds of sources like enterprise systems, other documents, or the Web. The service compositions evolve over time as services are called, delivered, added, or removed. Offering documents themselves as services enables their use and reuse in other tools and collaborations. The composition of services into a document is driven by coordination mechanisms which enable interactions between participants and manage dependencies in collaborative document creation. Participants are enabled to define appropriate coordination means for their specific collaboration scenario.

In order to proof the hypothesis, two main contributions are presented in this thesis: (a) a novel collaboration model considering the nature of collaborative document creation and (b) a collaboration system mapping the collaboration model on a software architecture. Figure 1.2 depicts an overview of the *collaboration model*. The collaboration model comprises five parts building on each other as outlined in the following.

(a) *Component Model*

In the component model the fundamental elements of a collaboration based on and targeted towards documents are identified. The objective of the component model is to provide a *uniform representation of human and non-human service providers* and their service types. Providers are potential participants of a collaboration offering resources and services.

(b) *Composition Model*

The composition model on top of the component model allows for the *representation of document evolution and refinement*. The composition model specifies how human coordinators can compose activities of participants (i.e., content provisioning and transformation) and delivered results into an evolving, hierarchical document. The objective is

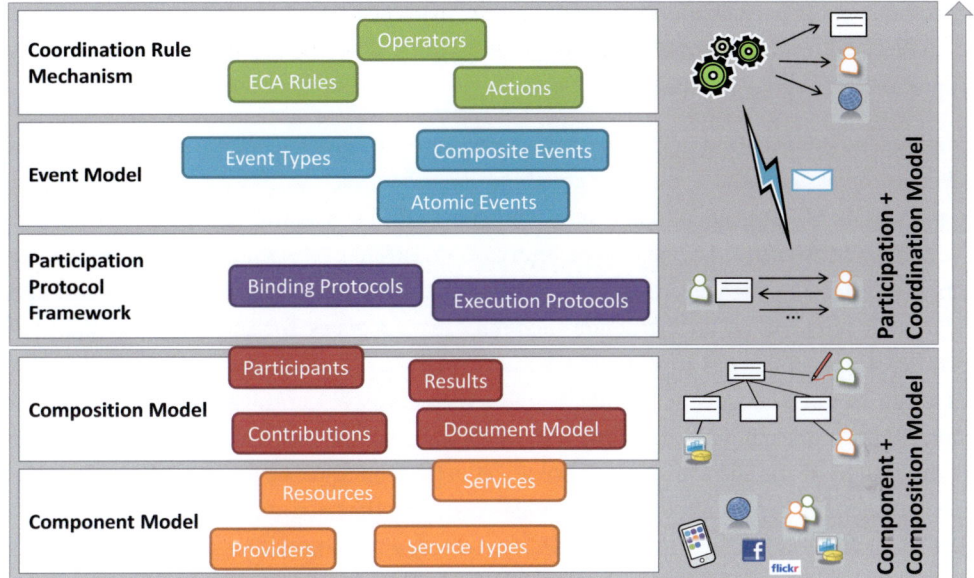

Figure 1.2.: Overview of collaboration model.

to provide a novel mechanism for end-users to flexibly compose resources and activities into one document.

(c) *Participation Protocol Framework*

The participation protocol framework enables the definition of *participation protocols* for interactions between a coordinator and participants of a collaboration including service binding and service execution protocols. The objective of the participation protocol framework is to enable the flexible selection of protocols according to the use case requirements. A set of protocols is presented which support different collaboration scenarios.

(d) *Event Model*

The event model *defines atomic and composite events* which might occur during collaboration, i.e., changes of the service composition and execution of participation protocols. The event model is extensible in order to be adaptable to a range of use cases.

(e) *Coordination Rule Mechanism*

An *event-condition-action (ECA) rule mechanism* enables participants to specify rules reacting on events. Rules allow for coordination of collaborations, including the partial automation of participation protocols and the management of dependencies between activities and results. Frequent dependencies between activities are identified and rules are proposed to manage them.

The second contribution of this thesis is the design and implementation of the Web-based *collaboration system* which maps the collaboration model on a software architecture following paradigms of Representational State Transfer (REST). Central to REST is the notion of interlinked resources, i.e., pieces of information, offered through uniform service interfaces [146, p. 55] which makes this architectural style a promising realization candidate. The system provides an infrastructure including (a) a registry for service publication and discovery, (b) a persistency to store collaboration results, (c) a messaging component to support participation protocols, (d) a rule engine which enforces coordination rules, and (e) an adapter framework enabling developers to build adapters for external services. The architectural design of the infrastructure enables the implementation of a range of collaborative document creation applications as it provides configuration and extension points, e.g., for event and activity types, coordination rules, and communication channels for contributing to a collaboration. The collaboration application complementing the infrastructure provides a graphical front end for human participants of collaborative document creation.

The research procedure followed during design and development of collaboration model and system as well as an overview of the thesis structure are presented in the following.

1.3. Research Procedure and Thesis Organization

Advancing the state of the art is a main output of research. Finding answers to boolean questions allows for changing or advancing the body of knowledge as done in knowledge (or evaluative) research. Complementary, practical research (or developmental research or engineering) advances state of the art through designing and implementing solutions in order to change the world in a particular domain or for a particular stakeholder (see [92][148]). The work in this thesis is *practical research*, aiming for advancing state of the art in the area of service computing through developing a new or improved technology for coordinating service compositions which involve humans. This goal was pursued through following the research procedure depicted in Figure 1.3. The left hand side of the figure presents the phases followed throughout the thesis work. Results produced during these phases expand into the parts and chapters of this thesis as presented on the right hand side. In the following, the activities performed during the phases are described along with the contents of the parts and chapters of this thesis document.

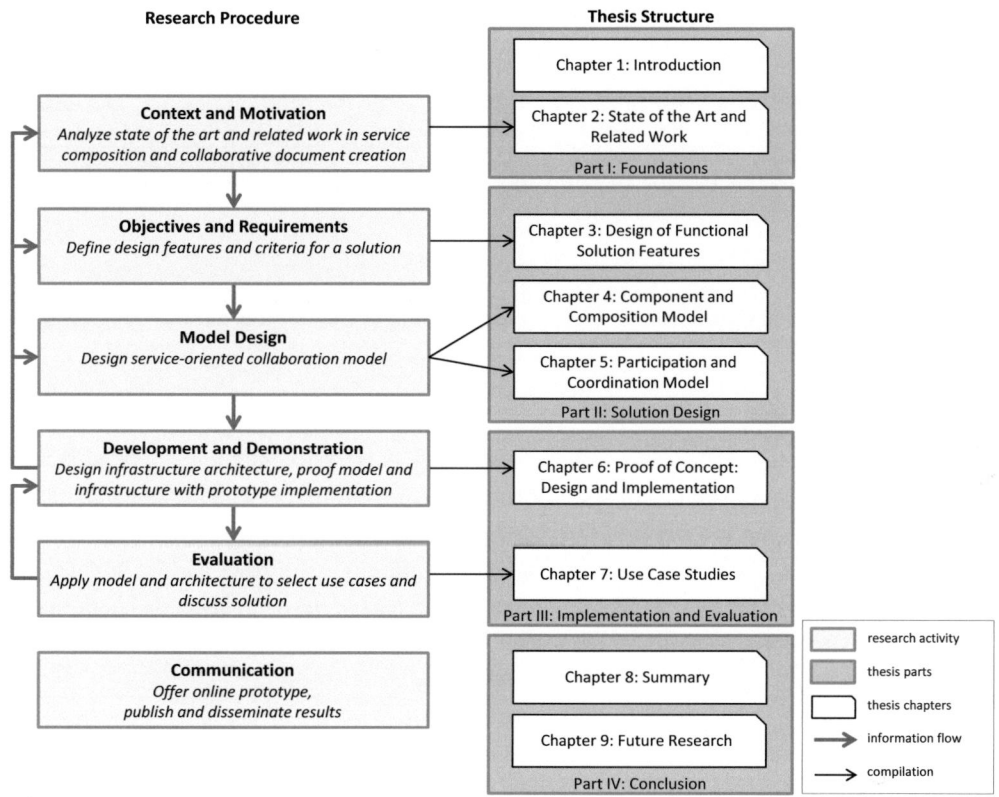

Figure 1.3.: Overview of research procedure and thesis structure.

- *Context and Motivation*

  In order to capture the research context as well as to motivate the relevance of applying service composition for collaborative document creation, state of the art and related
  work were investigated. Research and solutions in service composition as well as collaborative document creation were analyzed to cover a wide range of document types
  and collaboration processes and present a versatile approach. Discussing ideas and solutions throughout the thesis work in different related contexts like Web engineering,
  computer-supported cooperative work (CSCW), process flexibility, or SOC improved
  the understanding of the problem context and shaped the solution. The results are
  documented in Chapter 2. The chapter shows that leveraging service composition for
  human collaboration is novel and promising.

- *Objectives and Requirements*

  The context and motivation served as input for the inference of functional design features which serve as objectives and requirements for the solution design. The design features include fundamental elements of collaborative document creation, activities, coordination demands, and structure and format of target documents. The design features are presented in Chapter 3.

- *Model Design*

  Based on the design features, the service-oriented collaboration model was designed as outlined in Section 1.2. The solution design is presented in Chapters 4 and 5.

- *Development and Demonstration*

  In this phase, a collaboration system comprising an infrastructure and application was designed and implemented in a Web-based software prototype. The implementation of the system serves as a proof of concept for both, the architecture as well as the collaboration model. The design and and implementation of infrastructure and application are described in Chapter 6. The demonstration is part of the evaluation in this thesis as it proofs general feasibility of the research.

- *Evaluation*

  In the evaluation phase, the model and infrastructure were systematically applied to select pilot use cases in order to demonstrate use of the collaboration model and system for different kinds of collaborative document creation: participatory service design and community-driven pattern documentation. Chapter 7 describes the implementation of both use cases and the extensions they provide on the model as well as a discussion of the met objectives and requirements as defined in Chapter 3.

- *Communication*

  Parts of this work were disseminated in a set of peer-reviewed research publications which are referenced throughout this thesis. The implementation is offered as an online research prototype to the public.

All phases in the procedure were subject to iterations during the course of the work which led to refinements of the corresponding output. As noticed by the authors of [92], constructing a system and observing its behavior helps understanding the research domain. The iterations have led to cycles in the procedure followed in this thesis work represented by the information flow arrows with backward direction in Figure 1.3. For instance, the model design was incrementally refined also during the subsequent phases, e.g., the implementation.

As an example, a first version of the collaboration model involved a complex role model. The evaluation in example use cases like collaborative project proposal writing or the pilot use cases showed that a role model was not required.

The procedure resembles methodologies followed in *design science*, more precisely, the design science research methodology described in [109]. The design science paradigm focuses on practical research, notably on research which attempts to create or improve artifacts supporting humans in a specific domain (cf. [148]). Design science is in particular applied in information systems research where systems are implemented in the frame of an organization in order to improve "the effectiveness and efficiency of that organization" [57]. Central to design science is developing and evaluating artifacts like constructs, models, methods, or instantiations in order to understand a particular problem and proof solutions to this problem [57]. The focus in this thesis work is not the creation of an information system which has to integrate business strategy, organizational structure as well as IT infrastructure [57]. Still, artifacts – the collaboration model and system – are created and evaluated which involve people, technologies, structures and work systems as do information systems which makes the design science a suitable analogy.

2. State of the Art and Related Work

Composition, collaboration, and coordination – the keywords of this thesis – are brought together in this chapter. Service *composition* is a mechanism to build flexible and scalable software for manifold application areas. Human *collaboration* is inherently flexible and often results in composed documents which evolve over time through ad hoc interactions. *Coordination* is important for both, composition and collaboration: coordination mechanisms help improving qualities of service composition executions and ensure correctness of conversations between services in service compositions. Similarly, coordination enables effectiveness of collaboration and improves quality of documents produced during collaboration. This chapter motivates the utilization of *coordinating service compositions* to support flexible collaborations resulting in a document. Related work as well as research gaps are presented.

As shown in Figure 2.1, the chapter starts with a discussion on service composition in Section 2.1 which presents related work as regards humans in service compositions, composition styles as well as flexible service composition. The section shows that service composition research lacks an approach for human-driven, flexible service composition.

Section 2.2 introduces the case of collaborative document creation. Collaboration environments support composition of documents as well as basic coordination of human activities. Support for the integration of non-human participants, however, is insufficient; the produced documents are of rather static nature – a fact that motivates the use of service composition for such applications. Section 2.3 presents a set of dependencies to be managed during collaborative document creation as well as how coordination mechanisms used in service composition can be applied to manage them.

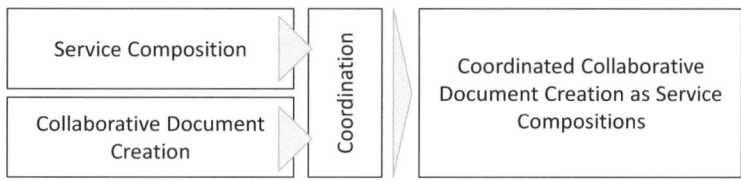

Figure 2.1.: Overview of state of the art.

2.1. Service Composition

Services are platform-independent autonomous distributed software-entities which perform functionality ranging from simple contents provisioning to complex business processes. Functionality is offered through a self-describing interface based on open standards to be invoked by other software programs over the Internet [103]. The nature of services ranges from enterprise applications to services delivering one piece of information on request. Enterprise services often comply to quality metrics, e.g., as regards availability, performance, or consistency. In contrary, services running on mobile phones or sensor-based services offering real-time data might act context-dependent, e.g., change quality of service based on the context.

The aggregation of services enables the provisioning of complex, distributed service-based applications to the consumer. The functional aggregation of services is called *service composition*. Service composition enables the the maximization of service reuse [68][53], the combination of functionality into a coherent larger service [7, p. 245ff.], or the creation of (short-lived) situational applications [153] designed to meet specific end-user needs [59]. Service composition is applied to support a large variety of applications on different kinds of devices. Figure 2.2 shows two exemplary applications. The (simplified) automated business process for flight booking in Figure 2.2(a) involves stable software services which are ordered and validated in a specification phase before being automatically executed. The example in Figure 2.2(b) is a service-based collaboration for content production involving services like content provisioning or translation. These services are composed and executed as needed during runtime of the service composition.

Services and service compositions can be realized using specifications of the Web services technology stack (WS-*). WS-* is a comprehensive set of partially standardized models and protocols originally developed to solve enterprise application integration problems and to enable the Web as communication channel for distributed applications [7, p. 93]. WS-* includes basic specifications for enterprise-level service-oriented architecture (SOA) like the Web Services Description Language (WSDL) [144] for the description of service functionality, SOAP for messaging [143], or languages for specifying and executing service compositions like the Web Services Business Process Execution Language (WS-BPEL) [95].

WS-* is an effort in the evolution of technologies supporting information systems distributed in or between business organizations, e.g., cooperative business processes. Quality aspects play an important role in the integration or composition of services in such systems. Therefore, a large number of complementary and interoperable specifications exist supporting quality aspects like reliability of messaging, transactionality, or security (cf. [146]).

The *standardization* efforts of WS-* helped spreading technologies without central coordination [7, p. 233], thus, fostering automation and interoperability. In addition, the WS-* tech-

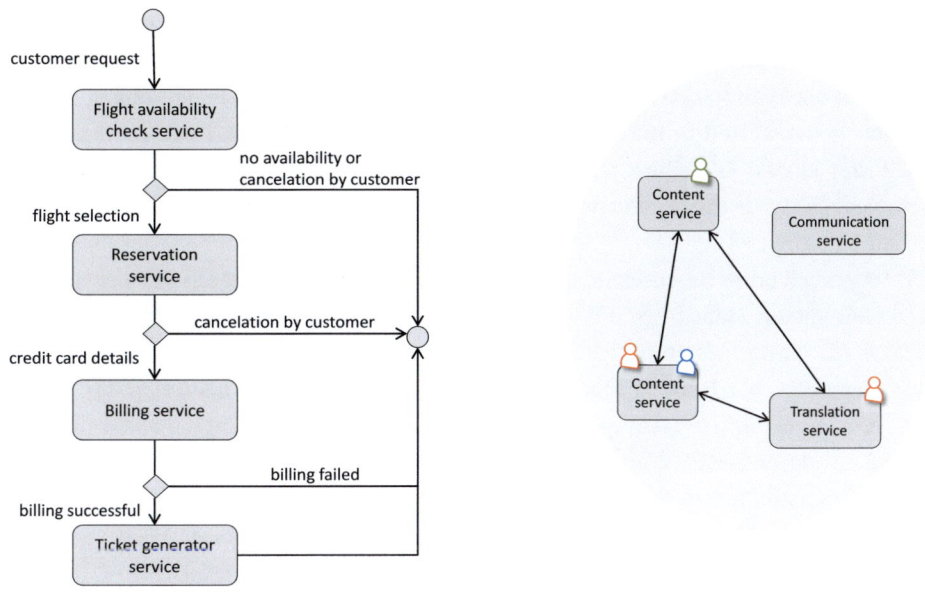

(a) Automated business process example.   (b) Service-based collaboration example.

Figure 2.2.: Example service-based applications.

nologies are accepted and implemented by many companies which has led to a large number
of frameworks and tools supporting developers in realizing Web services. These tools range
from source code generators to notations which allow developers to specify service compositions on a business level, e.g., Business Process Model and Notation (BPMN) [102], and
hide the complexity of the WS-* technologies from the developer.

Originally, the term *Web service* was coined for services realized with WS-* standards.
However, alternative implementation styles for Web services exist, e.g., REST. REST is an
architectural style for distributed hypermedia systems [47]. REST abstracts design decisions
of the Web. Central to REST is the notion of a *resource* which is a piece of information which
can be uniquely identified [146, p. 55] and addressed using a Uniform Resource Identifier
(URI). A service provides access to these resources offering a uniform service interface,
e.g., create, read, update, and delete (CRUD) in the Hypertext Transfer Protocol (HTTP). On
request, a service provides representations of the underlying resource.

In order to compose RESTful services, representations might be complemented with meta
data in form of hyperlinks. This data informs the client about valid state transitions in
the service-based application, i.e., which services in the composition can be called next
by the client. This principle is known as Hypermedia as the Engine of Application State

(HATEOAS) [47, p. 82]. Alternatively – or additionally – a service might aggregate resources internally, offering one central interface to the client.

A RESTful application does not store state of an interaction with a client, rather, all state
information is transferred in messages. If session state is not stored, a service can be re-
covered faster in case of failure which improves reliability of the overall application. In
addition, scalability of the application is improved because servers do not need to persist
session state [146, p. 55].

REST is perceived to be easier to understand than the WS-* technologies because it is
based on well-known, standardized Web technologies, but also, because less design decisions
are to be made during designing RESTful service-based applications. Perceived usability,
however, decreases if advanced functionality or quality criteria are needed [108]. REST
does not provide enterprise-level quality of service which has to be implemented manually
if required. In addition, RESTful services are restricted to the uniform interface to which all
required functionality has to be mapped.

To summarize, both, WS-* and REST, have strengths and weaknesses. Which approach
to use depends on the requirements of the application. The reader is referred to [108][156]
for a detailed comparison of the approaches as regards concepts and technologies.

Independent of the architecture and technology used to realize services and service compositions, a multitude of service composition models exist for supporting different types of
service-based applications. The examples in Figure 2.2 visualize three aspects of service
composition models which are of particular interest for this thesis and expose related work
examined in the following sections:

1. In service-based collaboration applications, *humans* are involved as service consumers
   and providers. State of the art for humans in service composition is outlined in Section 2.1.1.

2. The composition of services ranges from flows of activities to layout-oriented compositions of resources provided by services. How activities and resources are composed
   as well as dependencies between services can be specified is defined by *service composition styles* as presented in Section 2.1.2.

3. In service-based applications for collaboration, the required services can not always
   be specified in advance which makes *flexible life cycles* of service-based applications
   important. How flexibility is achieved in current approaches is shown in Section 2.1.3.

2.1.1. Humans in Service Composition

Humans are able to perform activities like transformation or computation or deliver information which can not be done by a software service. Collaboration or business processes

frequently require the participation of humans for example for approvals [100] or the delivery of contents. Through representing human activities as services, they can be more easily integrated and composed into work processes or collaborations which are realized through service compositions. In addition, human capabilities and produced content can be made explicit. The ability to reuse capabilities can be increased.

Composing software services and services provided by humans into service compositions results in *mixed service-oriented systems* [120]. Services provided by humans differ from software services in that their quality can not always be guaranteed, it might vary over time and depends on the application domain or the skills of a person. Therefore, the composition of different types of services performed by software and humans poses challenges on service composition approaches like the adequate representation of services, providing suitable user interfaces for service provisioning, enabling discovery of existing services, defining interaction protocols catering for human behavior, and enabling required trust [40].

Various approaches exist addressing these challenges. As part of WS-*, the WS-Human-Task specification [99] defines a human task as a service which is implemented by a person. The service-oriented representation of human tasks allows them to be used in different environments of different vendors (portability) as well as enables interactions of tasks which are distributed across environments (interoperability). The specification supports coordination mechanisms like reminders, the reassignment of tasks to other persons or groups during execution time, or the definition of completion conditions. The specification of tasks, however, has to be done by experts due to the complexity and multifaceted nature of tasks.

Based on WS-HumanTask, the WS-BPEL Extension for People (BPEL4People) [100] enables the integration of human activities into business processes. BPEL4People, however, uses the strict process-centric collaboration model of WS-BPEL which is not suitable for the composition and coordination of services in dynamic human collaboration for the creation of documents.

A research approach for the more flexible integration of human activities into service compositions is presented in [119][120]. The human-provided services (HPS) model and architecture allows for the design of personal services, the specification of tasks in a collaboration, and the selection of suitable HPSs responsible for executing these tasks. Alternatively, the availability of a task to be performed could be made public to the crowd and an interested person could volunteer to participate using its existing or a newly created HPS. A focus of HPS is on discovery and selection of services from the crowd based on social factors like reputation, expertise, or interests. Persons can create collaboration contexts and flexibly add activities to them which results in service sets controlled by interactions between humans and services [119, p. 25]. Accordingly, the HPS concept is applied for collaboration use cases like content sharing, ad hoc transformations, or business processes [121]. The composition of

HPS to simple process flows through pipes is supported in [139], where the micro-blogging service Twitter is used to coordinate communication between services and activities belonging to the same software migration project. Service compositions in this case are considered as *contexts* where services can be added as required rather than be specified in planned processes.

Human capabilities, e.g., encapsulated in HPS, can be composed to a Social Compute Unit (SCU) [39] representing capabilities of a team. SCUs are requested on demand to solve a specific problem and exist only for the required time, e.g., collaborative problem solving in a suitable team during incident management [130]. Like software services, SCUs can be discovered and composed, e.g., with software services. The composition of HPSs and SCUs with software services results in hybrid services, e.g., hybrid workflows, or in hybrid clouds which are able to scale as regards participating services [42]. In order to create hybrid clouds, the authors of [140] propose to represent human capabilities analogous to software service capabilities, e.g., exposing an application programming interface (API) or information on compute power, price, or location. On top of this representation, software developers can compose human-based and software services which can then collaborate to solve complex tasks.

While the approaches around HPS and SCU propose solutions for the composition of human-provided and software services, there is no approach for collaborative document creation involving the integration of results, e.g., documents, which evolve during collaboration.

Inspired by social communities and service marketplaces, the authors of [34] propose so called service communities which include sets of services contributed by community members on a per-project base. The concept does not prescribe which type of services are allowed in a service community and is therefore open to a large range of different service compositions including services provided by humans. While integrating social community features like tagging and communication services, the concept does not include a concept of composition of services which are part of a service community.

The authors of [67] describe the idea of utilizing human-provided services, called people services, in crowdsourcing scenarios. On request of a service consumer, a specialized platform aggregates a set of people services from an open set of volunteers. The platform coordinates the services in order to satisfy quality criteria of the requester, such as correctness of results or performance. Coordination mechanisms include selection of providers based on reputation, quality forecasting, or offering incentives to providers. Coordination can be performed based on requirements of a specific request. The platform, however, supports only crowdsourcing as organizational setting and accordingly does not consider collaborative document creation scenarios where participants collaborate or coordinators select specific services.

To summarize, existing approaches for the integration of humans in service compositions focus on the adequate representation of human activities in generic collaboration scenarios frequently inspired by social computing. The solutions are most often based on concepts and technologies of the WS-* stack, thus require detailed interface specifications for each service. A number of solutions allow for the composition of human-based and software services, however, lack composition models and coordination mechanisms in support of collaborative document creation. Similar to service communities and several composition models using HPS, a solution for collaborative document creation should consider a service composition as a set of human-based and software services which can be flexibly combined and coordinated as required during collaboration.

In general, service composition follows a composition style which specifies how services are logically composed. Several styles exist which are outlined in the following.

2.1.2. Service Composition Styles

A service composition style defines the kind of interdependencies which can occur between services in a service composition. Which service composition style is applied depends on the requirements of the realized service-based application. A traditional application field of service composition are business processes requiring a causal or temporal ordering between activities represented as services. Another example is the graphical composition of widgets involving services, e.g., weather forecast or stock market, on an integrated screen.

Once dependencies are defined according to a service composition style, they can be managed in order to improve quality aspects of a composition, e.g., consistency, efficiency, and performance. The management of dependencies is called *coordination*. Service composition styles are closely related to and interdependent with coordination as they define how and which dependencies can be specified. This section focuses on service composition styles. A more detailed discussion on coordination as defined in this thesis and coordination mechanisms is provided in Section 2.3.

A variety of service composition styles exist which can be characterized as *flow-based* and *resource* composition styles.

- *Flow-based composition styles* model the data or control flow in service compositions.

  Data flow styles focus on the correct data exchange between services. They can be realized through *wiring* of services in order to connect the output of one service to the input of another service, e.g., using pipes and filters [68], or through *event-based styles* which organize the composition around the exchange of events through messages. Services can subscribe for specific event types and get notified in case events of such types occur. This publish-subscribe communication style leads to concurrent processing which inhibits deterministic order of execution [19, p. 34]. There is usually no explicit control flow.

Control flow styles are frequently used for the automation support of business processes and borrow concepts and findings from the workflow automation domain [2]. Such styles enable the specification of a (partial) execution order among single service executions, also called orchestration. Realization variants of control flow compositions include complex workflows based on Unified Modeling Language (UML) activity diagrams or chart-like formalisms like petri-nets or π-calculus (see [7] for more details on these approaches). Another realization approach are *rule-based* systems based on events. Events serve as input for the specification of ECA rules capturing complex dependencies between services.

- *Resource composition styles* focus on the composition of resources provided by services in a composition. Service resources are frequently combined using grouping or layout-based styles.

  Grouping summarizes several services or service functions to a coherent one (cf. [68]) without establishing dependencies between them. An example for grouping is interface grouping, e.g., a composition of several search services returns a composition of all search results on request. Another example is the grouping of services by associating them to the same context, e.g., a project or service community.

  In the *layout-based* style, service output is ordered in a certain spatial representation and provides the impression of documents or dashboards.

A large body of research work exists in the area of service composition styles. For classifications and comparisons of service composition models using and combining different composition styles, the reader is referred to [27][41][64][68][137]. The majority of these publications focus on flow-based composition suitable for process-centric applications. Resource composition styles can be found in service mashup approaches using widgets for representing data from different services on one Web site, e.g., in the IBM Mashup Center[3], the composition of data-oriented services in portals for instance using the WS-* standard Web Services for Remote Portlets (WSRP) [97], grouping of related services in service communities [34], or grouping of HPS based on a collaboration context [139].

Combinations of both styles frequently occur. Many of these approaches, however, compose software services only. For instance, a layout-based composition is combined with an event-based composition to update the representation of a service based on an event (e.g., in the IBM Mashup Center[3]).

---

[3]http://www.ibm.com/developerworks/lotus/products/mashups/ (accessed January 2nd, 2013)

Another example is artifact-centric composition, where services are composed in a flow-based style and compose contents into (structured) business artifacts. Artifacts represent the progress of the service composition towards a business goal [60]. Similarly, case handling defines data objects as first-class citizens of a state-based process which can be used or filled with values by activities [4]. Case handling and most artifact-centric approaches require a model of the artifact before a composition can be executed. In collaborative document creation, however, the artifact can not be defined beforehand. A suitable combination of flow-based and resource composition styles for collaborative document creation is subject to research in this work.

Service composition styles define how dependencies can be defined between services and which dependencies can occur. A composition style, however, does not define *when* dependencies as well as other parts of a composition are defined. Service compositions supporting collaboration need to be flexible as regards the specification time of a composition. Approaches for achieving flexibility are described in the following.

2.1.3. Flexibility in Service Compositions

A service composition follows a life cycle during which it is specified and executed. Various service composition life cycle models exist [132][152] describing the following phases: (1) a requirements elicitation phase, (2) the abstract definition of one or more compositions of activities including dependencies and the selection of one composition alternative, (3) a mapping of the selected composition on concrete services, and (4) the deployment and execution of the composition, potentially including service composition monitoring.

An abstracted service composition life cycle including concrete steps is presented in Figure 2.3. During the three *specification* phases (1)-(3) the service composition is defined. Once specified, the service composition can be *executed*, i.e., the services can be called as designed in the specification. Specification as well as execution can be done manually by a human, for instance, an expert or the end user, or automatically. Automated execution is performed by a composition engine, e.g., a workflow engine. Such engines support correctness and efficiency of the execution as well as enable monitoring and tracking abilities [7, p. 126] in order to relieve users from manual tasks like invoking services. Automated specification is not relevant in this thesis.

These life cycles are suitable to support classical *design-time* (or pro-active) service compositions which are modeled at a dedicated design-time [27], i.e., during steps (1)-(3). Specification at design-time is performed if a service-based application requires an elaborate and reliable design by an expert before the service composition is executed, e.g., production workflows, but also if service compositions are automatically generated by an algorithm.

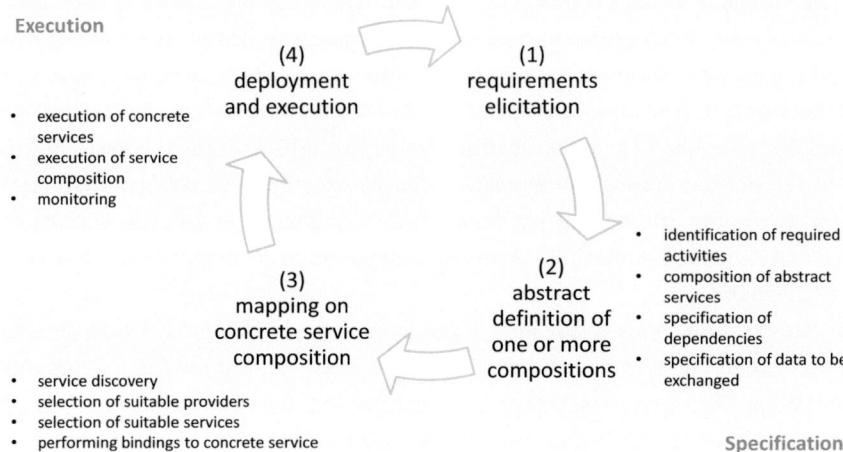

Figure 2.3.: Abstracted service composition life cycle with separated specification and execution phases.

Often, such compositions are required repeatedly in their form, for instance for business processes. Design-time compositions in general involve stable services.

Applications exist, however, which require a *flexible* (or *semi-structured*) service composition, e.g., partial temporal ordering of services in a composition. User requirements might change during execution of the composition or new requirements might occur, selected services might become unavailable, new and better services might appear. Especially the service environment on the Web is highly dynamic and continuously changing. Services might be removed, change their interfaces or new services might be added. Service compositions involving dynamic services need to flexibly cope with this dynamic service environment as well as changing requirements of the consumer [27].

Flexibility in service compositions frequently is reached through (a) performing quick cycles in the classical life cycles which is done in so called situational service compositions, (b) soften the phases prescribed by the life cycle by moving specification tasks of one phase to the next, or (c) using a composition style which comes with inherent flexibility during execution time. Which approach to flexibility is suitable depends on the application requirements.

(a) *Situational* (or ad hoc) service compositions are dynamically created on demand of a service requester. Such situational compositions are specified during quick cycles of design and execution phases similar to iterations in agile software development. Situational compositions are useful if there are only few requests for the composite service in its particular form or if some of the contained services are not stable [27]. Situational service compositions can be considered as evolving, situational systems which are flexibly adapted to changing needs. Examples for such compositions can be found in *service mashups* which enable end-users to compose (dynamic) resources from the Web into new applications which are created to be just as good as required and specifically serve a situational purpose [153]. Similarly to mashups, the mashup tool environment itself exposes a dynamic nature as new tools come to the market and other ones disappear. Since mashups are not intended to support long-running, transactional processes, service composers do not necessarily need to consider complex requirements like maintaining consistency or correctness. Steps in the service composition life cycle covering these aspects are skipped. Situational composition styles can also be found in the dynamic environment of ubiquitous computing [18].

(b) In order to support flexible service compositions, the steps performed during specification of a composition can be shifted to a later point in time. Softening the phases results in *execution-time* service compositions in which specification steps like activity specification, service selection or binding, as well as dependency specification can be done while the composition or parts of it are executed. A large research community, mostly originating from workflow research, focuses on the adaptability of designed compositions of activities, especially on the support of flexible business processes, not necessarily implemented with service compositions. Flexibility generally is achieved through enabling adaptability of modeled compositions as well as allowing late specification of parts of the composition [145]. For studies on achieving flexibility in, mostly process-oriented, compositions of activities, the reader is referred to [145][22].

Solutions for flexibility in service compositions frequently are also influenced by workflow research. Several solutions use or extend WS-BPEL. Approaches for adaptability include the ability to add new activities to a process or change dependencies between activities [145]. Late specification is realized through replacing an abstract task through a concrete implementation at execution-time based on the execution context [5], dynamic service selection [25] leveraging automated interpretation of user requirements [53], dynamic service binding [65], or the partial definition of composition models, e.g., using templates [118] or generic nodes [25]. Since these approaches are independent of the composition style, they are applicable to both, flow-based and resource service compositions.

A study of approaches to achieve flexibility in flow-based service compositions is presented in [64]. The study shows that flexibility as regards changes to process models or instances like late specification or service selection at execution-time is well supported in current approaches. In such compositions, flexibility highly depends on the way how flexible the relationships between the used services like constraints, mutual obligations, or agreed performance levels are specified. Changes of relationships between services or service interfaces still pose challenges on such process-oriented compositions [64].

(c) Using declarative or event-based composition styles enables intrinsic flexibility abilities. For instance, the composition style in case handling enables the automated execution of services as soon as they can be executed and not based on a pre-defined activity flow [4]. Rule-based composition styles are declarative and provide a higher level of modularization [63] than graph-based composition and therefore allow for the definition of more flexible workflows [81], e.g., when applied to change flow dynamically during run-time [31]. The maintenance overhead, however, is higher since the composition is implemented in a decentralized manner.

Although a large body of research exists for supporting flexible service compositions, no solution could be found for supporting collaborative document creation. Existing approaches either use a flow-based approach neglecting the need for resource composition, or they require the specification of particular model parts, e.g., dependencies, in a too early phase which makes them too rigid for supporting human collaboration. Resource service compositions which aggregate services based on their membership to a context like in HPS collaborations or service communities can be considered flexible as they enable adding or removing services as required. Human collaboration, however, often requires a mechanism to specify dependencies between tasks which is not provided by these approaches. Therefore, this thesis aims to find a suitable flexible life cycle for supporting collaborative document creation which still allows for the definition and coordination of dependencies.

Service composition caters for a large range of applications. In this thesis, collaborative document creation should serve as an application for completely new types of service composition. In the following section, the application and its existing support is discussed in more detail.

2.2. Collaborative Document Creation

Collaborative document creation is a multifaceted case. Different collaboration scenarios expose varying requirements as regards document models, participants and their contributions, communication, or coordination which need to be considered in collaboration systems. In order to qualify the scenarios addressed in this thesis, the following sections describe (a) modern electronic documents as compositions of potentially distributed material in Section 2.2.1, (b) the nature of creation processes of such documents in Section 2.2.2, and (c) state of the art and related work for collaborative document creation support in Section 2.2.3.

2.2.1. Electronic Documents

Since documents already existed before computers and the Web were invented, the understanding of the term *document* evolved over time. Formerly, documents were understood to capture textual notes.

Modern electronic documents can be defined as units "consisting of dynamic, flexible, nonlinear content, represented as a set of linked information items, stored in one or more physical media or networked sites; created and used by one or more individuals in the facilitation of some process or project." [122]. Documents allow for the integration of additional document structures and content sources and types [20], evolve over time, and can be copied, split into parts, and reused in various contexts. Kinds of documents range from transactional to narrative, they might be targeted to humans (e.g., documentation) or computers (e.g., source code) [52, p. 10f.]. New kinds of display devices and technologies, e.g., user interfaces like speech or touch, change the experience of documents [101].

Documents in the Web age are *compositions* of potentially distributed and related material in order to provide a uniform, purposeful view to the reader. The components are composed and structured on content, behavior, and representation level.

- The *content* which is composed in documents might stem from *different sources*, e.g., from humans, enterprise systems, or the Web. Especially the Web opens up the possibility to produce new kinds of documents involving unforeseen kinds of content, possibly composed on demand at time of representation. This content might have different media types and be subject to frequent changes which can not be controlled by the original document authors. For instance, multimedia or hypermedia documents like Web sites or mashups might involve data formats like videos, animations, or real-time data, e.g., contributed by sensors. Documents might include user-created contents like annotations, links, or comments which leads to the impression of a document ecosystem rather than single documents [101]. The analysis of typical documents in various domains like software engineering or research showed that the content in the produced documents usually follows a particular logical *document structure*, which possibly evolves during collaboration [129] and depends on the type of document to be produced as well as the language used in the document, e.g., spoken or visual. A common structure is a tree or hierarchy which can be found in many written documents which are decomposed into chapters and sections, like books, technical documentation, or project proposals. Another example structure is history-based like a forum thread.

- A document might include *behavior* like temporal models, user navigation models, or rules which are part of a document. A temporal model [15] captures temporal interdependencies between the elements in the document. For instance, in a presentation

multiple slides are presented one after the other, connected through sequencing relationships. Hyperlinks allow authors to link documents or parts thereof and thus enable
navigation interactions for controlling the flow, e.g., in a presentation [15]. Transactional documents like forms might be exchanged in a structured business process, allow for information reuse in steps of a business process as well as include rules which
might automate processes [52, p. 20ff.].

- A document also has a *representation* which includes formatting and fonts and is important for narrative documents targeted to a human audience. The document structure
  is persisted, i.e., mapped to a physical structure or spatial model which describes the
  arrangement of visual objects on the presentation screen [15]. This can be done in pro-
  prietary or standard *document models* like XML or HTML. Tools like Web browsers
  or word processors render various document models to create a uniform document
  experience.

Orthogonal to the content, behavior, and representation levels are *functionalities* which are
associated with documents. Important functionalities are document management services
like backup, version control, synchronization, notification of updates, or application-specific
functionality like workflow, format, or presentation transformations. Functionality might
also include the management of a document life cycle which involves activities like review,
approval, or discussion performed by different participants. In addition, documents or parts
thereof – including incorporated functionality – need to be *reused* on various levels of gran-
ularity [15]. Documents might be reused as they are or modified before reuse. Reuse enables
the incremental change and evolution of documents [77] and leads to building variants and
versions of documents which need to be managed.

Functionalities for document management can be supported by specialized tools or environments as presented in Section 2.2.3 or be directly included into documents making them
active. For instance, in [36], active properties including programming code for document
management can be injected into document operations or associated with whole documents.
Specific document models for the composition of hypermedia documents exist [46] which
enable reuse of media artifacts and higher level concepts like layout information or adaption
rules.

The Web offers an increasing number of services implementing such functionality, e.g.,
on-the-fly translations of documents or formatting. The Web also enables evaluation and
feedback for pieces of information by a large community, e.g., through social networks. Such
functionality is already incorporated into open Web-based knowledge bases like Wikipedia
and also proposed for "liquid publications" in the research domain where paper-like static
documents are still a daily occurrence [24].

The creation and evolution of documents frequently is done in teams, groups, or by the crowd. A number of services, tools, and collaboration environments exist supporting different aspects of collaborative document creation like document composition, content integration, or coordination. The nature of collaborative document creation as well as existing tools are outlined in the following sections.

2.2.2. Collaborative Creation of Electronic Documents

Collaboration can be defined as "the act of working together on a common task or goal", as opposed to working independently [14, p. 3]. Persons participate in a joint working process [71, p. 20]. In a *cooperation* people are operating towards a joint goal or benefit, as opposed to competing [14, p. 3][1]. Cooperating individuals produce a joint result, e.g., product or service [71, p. 21]. The terms cooperation and collaboration are often used interchangeably [14, p. 3][71, p. 21].

The focus of this thesis is on processes and activities where people perform together on a common task (collaborate) in order to produce a joint result (cooperate). Collaboration and cooperation both happen. In this thesis, the term collaboration is used as an umbrella term for these kinds of activities. Collaborative document creation is a form of collaboration where the *goal* of the participants is manifested in one or more electronic documents. As opposed to a goal, which is the desired realization of a certain state, an *outcome* is the actual realization [14, p. 14]. During collaboration, several outcomes might be produced. The outcome of collaborative document creation are the actually created documents.

Collaborative document creation has been studied over the last couple of decades, especially in the area of collaborative writing and collaborative software development. The advantages of collaborative vs. individual document creation include the improvement of document quality, e.g., regarding mistakes, understandability and accuracy, as well as the ability to integrate and transfer various viewpoints, opinions, insights, and expertises (cf. [66][80][90]). Documents serve different purposes like being official contracts, documenting circumstances, representing real-world aspects, capturing common understanding of a fact, or enabling knowledge transfer. Thus, collaborative document creation and evolution can be found in manifold parts of an organization or everyday life, for instance in education, knowledge management, software engineering [147], IT management [79], or research [66]. Created document types range from written papers (e.g., business plans, specifications, requirements documents, bug reports, meeting protocols), graphical models serving as visual representations of an aspect of the real world (e.g., architectural design models), to Web sites or source code.

Collaborative document creation is an inherently social and iterative process [80] which includes ad hoc or creative human interaction and is often driven by knowledge. While the

outcome is clearly defined as a joint document, the nature of collaborative document creation
as regards team size or group organization, as well as coordination of activities and participants varies to a large extend. Like contents is distributed over different sources, tasks are distributed among team members. During collaboration, participating humans plan, coordinate
activities, discuss, and negotiate which requires communication. The tasks to be performed
during document creation can only roughly and tentatively be planned in advance [74]. During collaboration, communication and resource exchange between participants might lead to
changes in plans or tasks [71]. Still, coordination mechanisms are applied in order to enable
effectiveness and improve quality of documents produced during collaboration. For example, a popular strategy during collaborative writing is the splitting of documents into parts
and assigning those parts to different participants [110]. Additional coordination mechanisms
are outlined in Section 2.3. Several tools and environments exist, supporting participants in
composing documents or coordinating dynamic collaboration processes as described in the
following.

2.2.3. Collaboration Tools and Environments

Collaborative document creation requires tools and environments which enable composition
of documents and integration of distributed, heterogeneous, reusable, and potentially dynamic resources into documents. Concurrent access to documents as well as dependencies
between activities need to be coordinated during collaboration in order to improve efficiency.
Accordingly, in the following, tools and environments for collaborative document creation
are examined as regards their composition and integration as well as coordination capabilities.

Collaboration systems are often summarized under the term *groupware* which are "com-
puter-based systems that support groups of people engaged in a common task (or goal) and
that provide an interface to a shared environment" [44]. Collaboration systems often are
intended to exist as supplementals to off-line communication like face-to-face meetings or
phone conferences. Essentially, groupware for collaborative document creation provides a
common information space or workspace – an environment – for the team which allows
participants to access and modify joint documents [71, p. 46f.]. Document management
systems like Alfresco[4], version control systems like Git[5], or file shares like Dropbox[6] enable
storing and sharing of documents belonging together in a project space. These environments,
however, allow for composition on the project space level rather than of documents which
might integrate heterogeneous contents. Reuse of document parts becomes cumbersome.

---

[4]http://www.alfresco.com/ (accessed January 2nd, 2013)
[5]http://git-scm.com/ (accessed January 2nd, 2013)
[6]http://www.dropbox.com/ (accessed January 2nd, 2013)

Although a large number of document models provide a hierarchical document structure or enable integration of multimedia, only few environments exist directly supporting the collaborative *composition* and *integration* of heterogeneous content from different sources. An early approach for collaborative editors are collaborative compound document environments as defined in [138] which compose editor instances including contents of different media types. These editors might support different kinds of collaboration for a specific media type. The approach focuses on the composition and extension of (collaboration) editors rather than on content composition or the coordination of human activities during content composition. The authors of [16] describe a framework for supporting users to retrieve and compose heterogeneous multimedia content resources from potentially arbitrary content sources into documents. However, while resources can be shared with others, nothing is said about support for collaborative creation of resources or composite documents. Similarly, mashup environments [153] allow for the composition of resources from the Web like data or user interfaces into dashboard-like, dynamic documents which include always up-to-date information. For example, with Yahoo!Pipes[7] users can combine several feeds into one feed. However, as mashup approaches most often focus on situational and personal applications as opposed to collaboration, they do not support coordination and human interaction.

Regarding *coordination*, a frequent feature of several mostly Web-based document production environments is the management of concurrent access to documents or document parts. Such environments can be distinguished into

(a) asynchronous environments implementing version control and pessimistic or optimistic locking strategies on resources,

(b) synchronous environments allowing participants to access and modify the same document simultaneously, and

(c) multi-synchronous environments which are able to switch between both styles during collaboration [51, p. 162ff.].

Examples for asynchronous environments are version control systems like Git or Subversion[8] which are used by large distributed teams of software developers. Version control systems provide a centralized document repository which enables traceability of changes as well as conflict resolution mechanisms in case of parallel changes on documents. A decentralized approach for storing composed documents is implemented in E-Breaker [9], an environment for collaborative software development. During development, participants decompose source code into pieces and assign them to owners. Code pieces are stored locally at each participant and synchronized in order to enable asynchronous collaboration. Version control systems are

---

[7]http://pipes.yahoo.com/pipes/ (accessed June 19th, 2012)
[8]http://subversion.apache.org/ (accessed January 2nd, 2013)

often utilized for the creation of other documents than source code like documentation or
research publications [90]. MediaWiki[9], on which Wikipedia is based, enables asynchronous
collaborative writing on one document avoiding conflicts of parallel writing using an optimistic concurrency control. Examples for synchronous Web-based tools are Google Docs[10],
Zoho[11], or typewith.me[12] which allow for real-time collaborative editing of rich text documents or spreadsheets. Such environments allow users to see what others see and do.

Coordination for concurrent access on the data level is well supported. A number of environments support additional application-centric collaboration features for coordination like
sending notifications on updates [76][75], commenting on document or parts of it (e.g., in
Google Docs, MediaWiki), or reminders on tasks [76]. In several environments, the assignment of activities to participants is used to support higher-level coordination. An early
example, Quilt [76], uses role models for the management of permissions on activities on
the document like editing or reviewing. Similarly, E-Breaker [9] supports the assignment of
document parts, i.e., code fragments, to responsible participants as well as the flexible del-
egation of the ownership to other participants. Quilt and E-Breaker, however, do not cater
for the management of dependencies between activities. Management of lightweight collaboration processes like travel approvals through the integration of several sources into one
document is realized in [75]. Workflow management support systems allow for more sophisticated process-oriented coordination of the creation of a document, e.g., orchestrating the
completion of a pre-defined form [17]. Such process-oriented tools, however, become too
rigid to enable human collaboration as described above. Most approaches do not consider
document compositions and reuse of document parts.

In order to support more flexible social workflows, e.g., during collaborative project report
creation, the authors of [35] propose to map human collaboration to software architecture
concepts. More precisely, human computation and data management activities are mapped
to (human) components; (human) connectors coordinate interactions between components.
Three collaboration patterns – social networks, shared artifacts (e.g., in Wikis), and crowdsourcing – are modeled using components and connectors and the flexibility of the patterns as
regards adaptations during collaboration is discussed. While the authors show that different
adaptation strategies required in collaboration can be reached in collaboration patterns, they
do not consider integration of non-human participants or specialized coordination mechanisms for collaborative document creation.

Existing tools and environments are suitable for particular phases in a collaboration process [10], meaning, they typically only support a limited set of interactions and limited co-

---

[9]http://www.mediawiki.org/ (accessed January 2nd, 2013)
[10]http://docs.google.com/ (accessed January 2nd, 2013)
[11]http://docs.zoho.com/ (accessed January 2nd, 2013)
[12]http://typewith.me/ (accessed January 2nd, 2013)

ordination thereof. For instance, in order to create a project report, a distributed team uses a group scheduling tool to find a suitable date (coordination). The discussion on the report is performed using a telephone conferencing system or e-mail (communication). Finally, the deliverable is collaboratively written using a real-time editor (co-production). Though several specialized environments for collaborative document creation exist, collaboration participants often use classical word processors made for single use and exchange documents for collaboration through e-mail or a version control system [90]. The benefit of using specialized collaboration environments for document creation might not be obvious to them (cf. [90]).

Collaboration tools and environments often are unintegrated which might result in error-prone content copy-and-paste activities from one tool environment to the other. In addition, using unintegrated tools hinders coordination, e.g., distribution of activities based on document parts, and reuse since such environments often use different document formats. Another reason might be that environments integrating different features like coordination and content production most often do not consider the user's existing tool environment. Individuals have to learn new tools other than their word processor which hinders adoption.

Statelets, an approach to coordinate collaboration across multiple collaboration tools is proposed in [78]. Statelets is a programming language which offers developers to integrate multiple software systems, e.g., groupware tools or social network services, which are used during a collaboration process. The language allows developers to specify coordination rules which consider context information (e.g., activities and participants in related projects) and execute actions according to process phases or context (e.g., trigger a call of a groupware API or e-mail to a particular participant). While coordination rules can be flexibly defined for a specific use case, the approach does not consider coordination of atomic tasks during collaborative document creation where content is integrated into a document.

This work aims at providing a first approach for supporting the composition and integration of heterogeneous, potentially dynamic contents from different sources while allowing participants to use their favorite editor or communication channel. In order to support coordination during collaborative content composition, a generic approach for integrating coordination mechanisms is investigated. A large set of coordination mechanisms exist for different purposes. In the next section, a relevant set of dependencies and coordination mechanisms is described.

2.3. Coordination

The term *coordination* is applied in several disciplines like computer science, organizational theory, artificial intelligence, or psychology. Abstracting from those domains, coordination can be defined as the management of dependencies between activities and resources [28]. Without interdependencies, there is no need for coordination [84][70].

Coordination is closely related to composition since through composition, dependencies between activities and resources are defined in order to create a coherent whole. Coordination allows for the management of dependencies in order to improve quality aspects of those composed systems. Quality aspects include system characteristics like efficiency, consistency, correctness, or performance. Coordination mechanisms can be automated in order to reduce the human effort for coordination [123]. Coordination not only focuses on the process of achieving a result but also might improve the quality of the outcome of a process itself, for instance a document in a collaboration application.

Literature on WS-* distinguishes the terms composition and coordination [7, p. 250ff.]. The implementation of a service is done using service composition styles. The implementation often is *internal*, since it is hidden from clients. Coordination protocols are used to precisely define allowed interactions with a service or between multiple services in order to guarantee correctness and consistency of the service execution and involved data. Accordingly, coordination protocols are coordination mechanisms which manage the *external* interactions which are important for design-time service discovery and execution-time service binding and thus need to be publicly visible [7, p. 205]. The order of invocations of services in compositions has to comply to coordination protocols. The composition decides on the possible conversations. Therefore, Web service technologies often support both, coordination protocol specification and composition definition. For instance, with WS-BPEL the internal execution implementation can be specified as well as the external protocols supported by the implemented service. Vice versa, in [135] an approach is presented to compose services talking certain coordination protocols using the WS-BPEL composition model. As part of WS-*, WS-Coordination is a framework for coordination protocols [96]. WS-Coordination allows services to register as participants in coordination protocols as well as to establish a context for an activity which follows a certain coordination protocol. The framework is protocol independent and can be extended with required protocols, e.g., atomic transactions with WS-Atomic Transaction [94] or WS-BusinessActivity for complex business processes [98].

In this thesis, coordination is understood on a higher level than in service computing literature: coordination is any management of dependencies during all phases of the service composition life cycle. Accordingly, adequate coordination means need to manage dependencies (a) during specification of service compositions complementing service composition styles as presented in Section 2.1.2 and (b) between services during execution, e.g., through coordination protocols.

Lifting the meaning of coordination in service-based applications to a higher level enables the specification of additional coordination means for supporting humans during the creation of service compositions as will be shown in the following sections. The goal in this thesis is to support an extensible set of relevant dependencies for collaborative document creation through existing coordination mechanisms rather than finding additional dependencies or creating new coordination mechanisms. Therefore, a set of relevant dependencies in collaborative document creation as well as coordination mechanisms in the field of service composition are examined in the following sections.

2.3.1. Dependencies

Dependencies might exist between activities, between resources, or between resources and activities. Resources can be understood as anything used or affected by activities like materials, efforts, actors, or states [28]. Two types of dependencies occurring during collaborative document creation are examined in this thesis: temporal and resource interdependencies [114]. Figure 2.4 provides an overview.

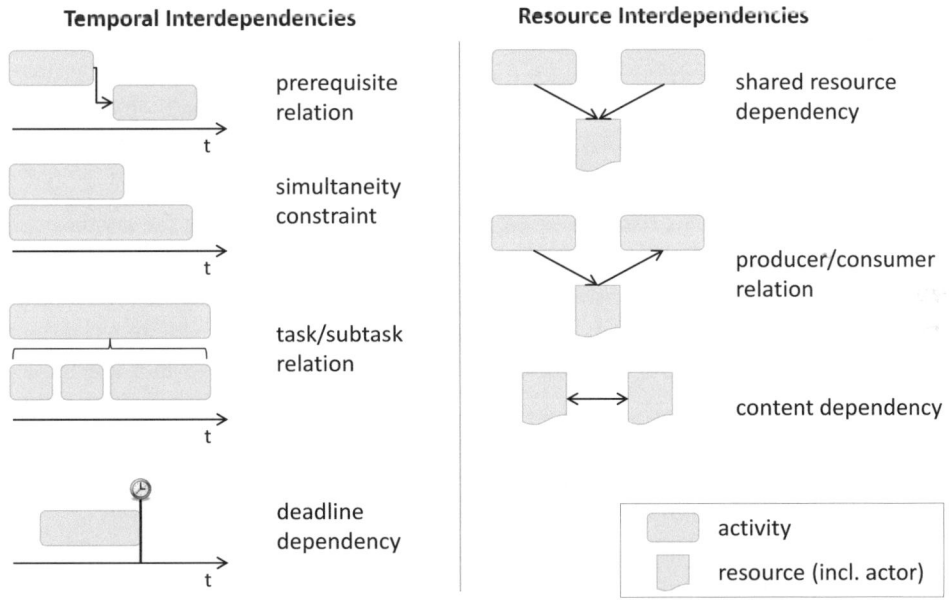

Figure 2.4.: Overview of temporal and resource interdependencies.

- *Temporal interdependencies* influence the order in which activities need to be performed.

  The prerequisite relation denotes that one activity can only be performed when a certain other activity is finished or that a resource needs to be produced before it can be used [114]. For instance, a proofread activity has to be performed on a project proposal before the document can be published or a language translation can only be done if the text is written.

Simultaneity constraints prescribe that two activities need to execute at the same time [84], e.g., synchronous collaboration is required.

A task/subtask relation exists if a set of tasks are required to fulfill an overarching task [84], for instance, in order to provide a diagram on an issue, a data acquisition task as well as a visualization task is required.

A deadline dependency can occur if a document has to be produced before a certain deadline, for instance given by the institution where the project proposal is to be submitted.

- *Resource interdependencies* occur when resources are distributed among activities [114].

Shared resource dependencies occur if two or more activities use the same resource [84][114]. This resource could for example be a section which should be written or proofread by two persons at the same time. A shared resource might also be the participant executing an activity who has to perform other activities in parallel, i.e., a dependency exists between an activity and a participant.

A producer/consumer relation exists if one activity creates input for another activity [84], for instance, a proofread activity depends on a writing activity which provides a text as input in collaborative document creation. This dependencies includes the usability dependencies which denotes that the output of the first activity has to be usable for the second [84]. For example, the text has to be written in a language the proofreader understands.

The content dependency denotes that two or more resources are related as regards their content, e.g., a picture and its description.

A survey about research on dependencies in service composition is provided in [87]. Similar to the dependencies found in coordination of human work, the author summarizes existing dependencies to sequence dependencies (a service depends on the completion of execution of another service) and data dependencies (a service depends on data provided by another service). Sequence and data dependencies can be sorted into temporal and resource interdependencies, respectively.

On the one hand, dependencies might constrain how activities can or should be executed. Therefore, coordination mechanisms exist which aim to minimize dependencies or conflicts caused by dependencies. On the other hand, making dependencies explicit might provide opportunities, e.g., provide additional information or enable automation [28]. A set of relevant coordination mechanisms and how they are supported in service composition is presented in the following.

2.3.2. Coordination Mechanisms

Because of the generic notion of coordination, a large number of coordination mechanisms exist for different purposes in different use cases. Several mechanisms might target to the same generic coordination problem or might be used complementary for the same problem. In many cases, one mechanism can be used to improve a number of different quality aspects. For instance, mechanisms for traditional atomic transaction support aim to ensure atomicity and isolation of operations, as well as consistency and durability of data.

In human collaboration, dependencies are managed through explicit coordination mechanisms supported with tools or artifacts and implicitly through the knowledge of the task and team context [45]. For each collaboration, a different set of coordination mechanisms is suitable. The focus in this thesis is the support of explicit coordination mechanisms through coordinated service compositions. For example, service composition styles as introduced in Section 2.1.2 offer combinations of mechanisms suitable to specific scenarios. In the following, coordination mechanisms supported by service composition models or collaboration solutions are examined and classified regarding their support of the dependencies outlined in the previous section.

For the management of temporal interdependencies in service-based applications different mechanisms can be applied during execution of compositions.

- Prerequisite relations might block the progress of a composition. Most approaches in service composition (e.g., WS-BPEL) apply *sequencing* as coordination mechanism for automating prerequisite relations. Automation can also be enabled using *notifications* via publish/subscribe. For example, actors could be notified on released data locks or a successor of an activity can be notified about the completion of the activity. *Tracking* enables participants to inspect the current state of the execution [84] and react on changes in the execution. Tracking in service compositions can for instance be enabled through service composition monitoring approaches.

- Simultaneity constraints are supported through *scheduling* the parallel execution of services. Spatial composition styles, e.g., in mashups, might execute all services at the same time. Flow-based approaches like WS-BPEL support the definition of parallel execution sequences. If simultaneously executed activities access or modify the same resources collaboratively, *synchronization* mechanisms are required to manage this shared resource dependency. In collaborative document editing, synchronization can for example be realized through What You See Is What I See (WYSIWIS) mechanisms [134].

- Task/subtask relations in general can be managed through *goal selection* and *task decomposition* where an overall goal is decomposed into subgoals which are performed as tasks by participants [84]. Task decomposition is inherent to service composition, where each service performs one activity to meet a collaborative objective. For instance, spatial composition styles enable the decomposition of tasks, i.e., delivery of resources, based on a planned resource structure. *Division of labor*, a coordination principle in collaboration [110][80], is supported naturally through assigning different service providers to services in the composition.

- Deadline dependencies can be supported by service composition models through *scheduling* [86] as well as *monitoring* activities which enables to interfere in case the deadline might not be met. No service composition model could be found which supports *reminders* for services provided by humans.

Resource interdependencies can be managed as follows.

- Shared resource dependencies might violate consistency requirements of an application when causing lost updates or dirty reads. As described in Section 2.2.3, a number of different concurrency mechanisms exist addressing this problem in collaborative document creation. An extensive overview of standard and research coordination mechanisms for data consistency and recovery in service compositions is presented in [50]. The mechanisms include advanced *transaction* mechanisms, relaxed *locking* techniques, *data dependency analysis* as well as *modularization* strategies. The focus of the approaches presented in the survey is to ensure consistency or reliability in process-centric compositions where the "all or nothing" (atomicity) property is required. Besides modularization, these mechanisms therefore are suitable to only a limited extent for service-based collaboration support. *Assignment* of responsibilities for resources or tasks or *sequencing* of activities based on their association to resources are alternative coordination mechanisms for shared resource dependencies.

- Similarly to prerequisite relations, producer/consumer relations can be managed with *notifications*, e.g., updates of resources can be propagated to interested parties. In service composition models, producer/consumer relations often are solved through data flow approaches, i.e., *sequencing*. *Standardization* of formats enables usability and understandability of resources exchanged between producer and consumer [84]. Standardization of languages and protocols allows participants to interact independently of a coordinating or translating intermediary [7, p. 132ff.].

- Content dependencies are specific to collaborative document creation and therefore not considered in service composition approaches. The update of one resource might cause an inconsistent other resource. In general, content interdependencies can be supported through *notifications* if a resource is updated or *sequencing* for requesting an update of one resource if the other updates.

Table 2.1 shows an overview of the presented dependencies and coordination mechanisms based on the general coordination mechanisms provided in [84].

Table 2.1.: Dependencies and coordination mechanisms (extended version of [84]).

Dependency	Coordination Mechanism
Temporal Interdependencies	
prerequisite relation	sequencing, notification, tracking/monitoring
simultaneity constraint	scheduling, synchronization
task/subtask relation	goal selection, task decomposition, division of labor
deadline dependency	scheduling, monitoring, reminders
Resource Interdependencies	
shared resource dependency	modularization, transactions, locking, data dependency analysis, task and resource assignment, sequencing
producer/consumer relation	notification, sequencing, usability through standardization
content dependency	notification, sequencing

Coordination mechanisms applied during service composition focus on the execution phase. The coordination of the (collaborative) specification of service compositions has been considered in service engineering methods. For example, in [62], a design process is described for the collaborative creation of service compositions which considers negotiations of different stakeholders. The coordination of flexible, human-driven service compositions in order to support collaborative document creation, however, has not been studied.

2.4. Conclusion

Collaborative document creation involves the distribution of work on several human and non-human participants as well as the composition of produced results into a document. During collaboration, communication protocols and coordination mechanisms are applied depending on the requirements of the particular collaboration. Service-oriented technologies naturally seem to fit to support collaborative document creation, as they allow for flexible coordinated composition of loosely-coupled, distributed services. The previous sections, however, showed that several challenges have to be tackled as regards coordinating service compositions for collaborative document creation.

- Humans can be integrated into service compositions as discussed in Section 2.1.1. Potentially, an unlimited number of software services participate in a collaborative document creation process. A solution thus should be scalable as regards participants. The specification of a dedicated service interface for each service allows for precise definitions of service capabilities. The prescription of a uniform interface for all human and non-human services, however, might result in higher scalability as regards participants. The mapping of participants of collaborative document creation processes to a uniform interface is addressed in this thesis.

- Flow-based and resource composition styles exist as well as combinations of both to support structured or situational applications as shown in Sections 2.1.2 and 2.1.3. In collaborative document creation, resources need to be composed into a document as well as activities for delivering resources need to be flexibly coordinated. Existing service composition styles, however, often neglect the need for resource composition, or they require the specification of model parts in a too early phase making them too rigid for supporting collaborative document creation. A style supporting collaborative document creation should allow service compositions to flexibly evolve over time as new services are added or executed and deliver resources. The design of such a composition style is tackled in this thesis.

- A number of coordination mechanisms allow for the management of dependencies between services, e.g., through notifications or sequencing, as shown in Section 2.3. Most of these mechanisms are applicable to the execution phase of a service composition and can potentially be applied for collaborative document creation. Collaborative document creation processes, however, require coordination mechanisms for the execution as well as the specification phase of a composition. In addition, different coordination mechanisms are required for different scenarios of collaborative document creation. The design of a solution for flexible coordination is addressed in this thesis.

In order to address the challenges, design features for a collaboration model based on service composition are derived as presented in the following chapter.

Part II.

Solution Design

3. Design of Functional Solution Features

The set of design features described in this chapter frame and demonstrate the concept of the solution which is provided by this thesis work. Section 3.1 defines which types of collaboration participants and activities are considered in this thesis in order to allow for a uniform representation of human and non-human participants. Section 3.2 introduces the mechanism allowing human participants to compose activities and created results into an evolving document. The specification of a composition can be coordinated based on the intended document structure. Section 3.3 provides a frame for communication protocols to involve participants depending on the use case. The protocols allow human as well as non-human participants to contribute to a collaboration. Finally, Section 3.4 describes the approach to enable flexible coordination of dependencies. The provided coordination mechanism is flexible as it can be extended and configured to suit to (a) a specific collaboration, e.g., through automation of a particular dependency, and (b) different use cases of collaborative document creation.

3.1. Activities and Participants

Activities performed by participants are the basic building blocks of a collaboration. The design features detailed in this section and summarized in Table 3.1 consider the nature of activities and participants in collaborative document creation.

During collaboration, participants play *roles* based on their abilities and expertise, or their position in the organizational hierarchy. Roles are associated with responsibilities and rights. Participants might perform several roles in a collaboration or change roles during collaboration [133]. In different use cases of collaborative document creation, different roles can be identified. For example, typical roles in collaborative writing are writer, consultant, editor, and reviewer [110]. The creation of models in systems or service design involves various stakeholders and experts like analysts, (service) providers, domain experts, and users [48][115]. During modeling, these stakeholders take different roles like modeler, facilitator, technical support, or gatekeeper (cf. [115] for a literature analysis about collaborative modeling as regards roles). These roles can be summarized to two basic roles: roles which are responsible for coordination and moderation of the group process and roles which are responsible for the content. The collaboration model therefore supports *coordinator and contributor roles* (DF 1-1). In the following, participants playing a coordinator role are called coordinators, participants playing a contributor role are called contributors.

Activities performed during collaboration include content production tasks like creating, refining, reviewing, approving, or publishing contents, performed by contributors, as well as coordination tasks like planning workflows, selecting participants, and division of work (cf. [80][110]). The collaboration model enables *human and non-human contributors*, i.e., software services, to execute content production tasks (DF 1-2) in order to enable dynamic and static data sources like sensors or data bases to act as contributors during collaboration. Software services like translators provide functionality or transform content. Both types of services, data and functionality, are supported by the solution.

Software services in general are heterogeneous in their nature, ranging from atomic to composite services. Activities can be considered atomic when they can not be subdivided. The contributions they can provide in collaborative service creation are restricted to atomic activities. As regards content production tasks, the collaboration model supports *atomic content production activities* (DF 1-3). The integration of complex services and activities is subject of future work.

Table 3.1.: Design features for activities and participants.

ID	Design Feature	Rationale
DF 1-1	Support of coordinator and contributor roles.	Coordinator and contributor are basic roles required in collaboration scenarios.
DF 1-2	Integration of human and non-human participants providing data and functionality.	More and more software services support humans in their daily work (cf. Section 2.2.1). Static and dynamic data sources act as content providers.
DF 1-3	Support for atomic content production activities.	Collaborative document creation involves content production tasks (cf. [80][110]).

A collaboration is considered as a composition of activities performed by humans and non-human service providers. The activities produce or refine content which is input to documents which incrementally evolve during collaboration. How content is composed is described in the following.

3.2. Content Composition

Through activities, participants contribute to a document which acts as a container for content. Several activities are performed by different participants over time in order to provide and refine document parts. Table 3.2 summarizes the design features for content composition which align composition of activities and content contributed by activities.

In order to coordinate the process of collaborative document creation, a goal selection and task decomposition mechanism is applied. The existence of a document for a specific purpose is selected as goal. Coordinators decompose the expected document into parts to be delivered or refined. Subsequently, coordinators can identify activities to be performed in order to create and update document parts. Activities are assigned to contributors following the division of work principle and the separate writers strategy as described in [110]. The process can, however, not be completely planned in advance and document structure and content evolve over time. The collaboration model therefore allows coordinators to *incrementally structure* a document over time, use the evolving structure to *identify tasks* as well as *integrate content* contributions into the structure (DF 2-1).

During collaboration, as introduced in Section 2.2.1, documents are composed on three levels: content, behavior, and representation. The composition of behaviors and representations as opposed to content composition was examined in other works like [21]. The behavioral model, e.g., a temporal model in a hypertext presentation, makes a document more complicated. As the document itself is not in the focus of this thesis, rather the collaboration and composition of contents and activities, the support of behavioral model composition is subject of future work.

The content in documents is composed following a document model or format, e.g., HTML, Office Open XML as used in Microsoft Office, or TeX. Modern documents involve dynamic contents of different types and structures [122]. Different types of document models and formats are used in different use cases. In addition, participants of a collaboration might use different tools for collaboration using different document models. In order to provide a solution for a range of collaboration types and allow participants to use their existing tool environment, e.g., a word processor or e-mail, the collaboration model is *document model independent* (DF 2-2).

Finally, documents or parts thereof – including incorporated functionality – potentially are *reused* as outlined in Section 2.2.1. Reuse in current document models of the Web often is difficult since the languages and models used do not separate content and representation. Thus, components or document structure can not be easily extracted. The collaboration model provides a possibility to reuse content independently of its representation as contribution to other documents (DF 2-3).

Table 3.2.: Design features for content composition.

ID	Design Feature	Rationale
DF 2-1	Enable incremental structuring of documents and mapping of activities and content to structure.	Structure evolves over time. Enables coordination mechanisms division of work and separate writers strategy.
DF 2-2	Independence of document model.	Different document models are used in different collaborations. Enable integration with user's tool environment.
DF 2-3	Support reuse of produced content.	Content might be interesting in other collaborations. Copy-paste is time-consuming and error-prone.

Required activities for content production and refinement are deduced from the evolving document structure. These activities can then be assigned to participants responsible to perform them. Once assigned, participants can start performing the activity. In the following section, design features for participation, i.e., assigning participants and performing activities, are described.

3.3. Participation

Participation is the execution of communication activities performed to integrate content into an evolving document. Activities are performed by coordinators and contributors. Table 3.3 summarizes the design features for participation.

Figure 3.1 presents a snapshot of a collaboration during the creation of a project proposal. The project proposal contains document parts specified by coordinators and associated with activities as described in the previous section. During collaboration, participants in the role of contributors are associated with the activities they are responsible for. In the beginning of a collaboration, not all required activities and potential contributors are known. Therefore, associating contributors should be possible any time during the collaboration. The association of a contributor and an activity can follow different protocols. For instance, a coordinator might search and find a suitable participant for an activity in a repository, e.g., an expert system or a repository of software services, and assign the contributor to the activity. In a project proposal project as exemplified in Figure 3.1, the team of contributors is clear which makes searching for a suitable contributor unnecessary. Another form of participation is applied in open source projects, where humans volunteer in performing activities. Therefore,

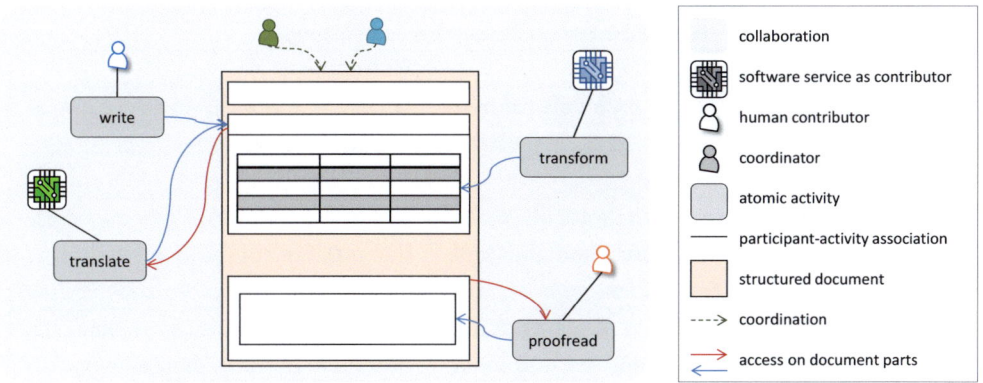

Figure 3.1.: Snapshot of collaborative project proposal creation.

the collaboration model enables a set of different *association protocols* which allow for finding contributors and associating them with an activity flexibly during collaboration (DF 3-1).
These protocols map on human interaction but are also understandable by software service
providers.

Having associated an activity and a contributor, the contributor can perform the activity
and create or refine one or more document parts. The contributor might start performing the
activity by itself or it might be asked to perform, e.g., by a coordinator. Activities possess
a *state*, e.g., started or executed. The execution of activities influences state of document
parts which might be delivered or refined. Making the state of activities and document parts
explicit enables the coordinators to track progress of the collaboration. *Execution protocols*
interrelate activity states with document part states and ensure correctness of activity executions as regards the states (DF 3-2).

Activities are performed in parallel by different contributors. Besides contributing contents, contributors might require to *access existing parts* of the composed contents. A contributor might be the consumer of content produced by another resulting in a producer/con-
sumer relation as described in Section 2.3.1. For instance, a translation service requires the
text to be translated as input. A person responsible for writing a summary requires the whole
document as context in order to provide an adequate contribution. The collaboration model
therefore stores documents centrally allowing write and read access to document parts to all
participants. Since not all parts of a document might be relevant to a participant or should be
accessed by the participant, a coordinator defines the parts to be accessed by the participant
during collaboration. (DF 3-3)

Table 3.3.: Design features for participation.

ID	Design Feature	Rationale
DF 3-1	Support different protocols for finding contributors and associating them to activities.	Different forms of involvement of contributors exist.
DF 3-2	Support execution protocols which associate execution of activities with document part states.	Support state tracking as coordination mechanism (cf. Section 2.3).
DF 3-3	Enable participants to access (parts of) the document and use it as input.	Participants might need to consume content to perform their activity.

Participation addresses the involvement of single contributors performing activities. In a collaboration, a team of participants works in parallel on the same goal which causes dependencies between activities. Design features for coordination mechanisms supporting these dependencies are presented in the following section.

3.4. Coordination

Participation looks at the single contributor who eventually delivers contents. Coordination is required, when considering a larger number of participants and potentially interrelated activities. As described in Section 2.3, a large number of dependency types exist in collaborative document creation which can be addressed by different coordination mechanisms. A set of coordination mechanisms is already applied through the design features described in the previous sections:

- Task/subtask relations are managed through decomposition of the document into parts which are associated with activities required to create and transform them.

- Association of activities to different contributors, i.e., task assignment, enables division of labor. Division of labor is a mechanism to avoid shared resource dependencies as regards time of participants. In addition, division of labor allows participants to work in parallel which speeds up the collaboration process [110][115].

- In order to enable coordinators to track progress of the collaboration, parts and activities possess a state which can be observed. Producer/consumer relations are supported through a blackboard approach which enables consumers to access all output created by producers.

The assignment of activities to different contributors throughout the collaboration and the parallel execution of activities which produce and consume contents of the same document, however, pose additional coordination requirements on the solution to manage producer/consumer relations, shared resource dependencies as well as content dependencies. Table 3.4 summarizes the design features to support coordination for these dependencies.

In order to provide one mechanism to enable management of many dependency types, the collaboration model defines an *extensible event model* (DF 4-1). Anything which happens during collaboration, e.g., the association of a new contributor, the identification of an activity, or the update of a document part, might be considered an event. Events serve as notification mechanism for producers who inform consumers about new input contents. Participants can subscribe to event types of other participants or document parts, e.g., to receive updates of a specific document part.

Listening to events and acting accordingly might become cumbersome for coordinators. In order to improve efficiency and reduce manual coordination effort, the collaboration model enables coordinators to *define rules throughout the collaboration* which allow for (semi-)automation of coordination mechanisms (DF 4-2). The solution enables coordinators to specify dependencies and rules specific for their collaboration, i.e., to tailor the coordination support according to their needs. For instance, the collaborative creation and infilling of a form possibly requires a controlled process whereas the writing of a scientific project proposal is more flexible without any specified process. Rules might automate the protocols for participation of single contributors, for instance, ask them to perform the activity as soon as they are associated with the activity. Sequencing as a coordination mechanism to manage prerequisite or producer/consumer relations or content dependencies can be automated through asking a contributor to perform an activity only after another activity is finished. Through events, inconsistencies can be avoided if coordinators are informed about potential inconsistencies when they are detected. Even not occurring events could be used to send reminders as a coordination mechanism for deadline dependencies.

Table 3.4.: Design features for coordination.

ID	Design Feature	Rationale
DF 4-1	Provide extensible event model to support notification as base coordination mechanism.	Coordination of dependencies enhances effectiveness [44] and potentially speeds up collaboration [110][115]. Notification supports a large set of coordination requirements.

Continued on next page

Table 3.4 – *Continued from previous page*

ID	Design Feature	Rationale
DF 4-2	Allow coordinators to specify rules based on events for different coordination mechanisms.	Rules enable automation which reduces manual coordination effort. Different use cases expose different coordination requirements.

3.5. Conclusion

The design features described in the previous sections capture the functional design of the solution. The design features integrate requirements and features extracted from the domain of collaborative document creation having service composition in mind.

A number of requirements in collaborative document creation are not considered in this thesis. Version control is an important feature to enable traceability and rollback. A large number of mechanisms exist for version control. In this thesis, however, traceability and version control are not examined. Support of transactions and exception handling in such collaborations is not provided by the collaboration model. Design and development of compensation logic is complex in workflow systems; in Web services, standards emerge [7, p. 272]. In the collaboration model, compensation logic partially can be managed by humans who might define specific rules. The same holds true for exception handling during the collaboration process. Transactions and exception handling on an infrastructure level is out of scope of this thesis. Security, e.g., through role-based access, is not realized in the solution. Security and role model requirements differ for each collaboration application. Selecting and applying suitable solution approaches is open to future work.

Understanding the semantics of documents which are (re)used in different contexts or by different persons is difficult as there might be various views and opinions which are not made explicit or missing background information. Therefore, face-to-face communication is still required in order to clarify document or document fragment meaning because direct communication allows participants to ask further questions as required [56]. The target of the collaboration model presented in this thesis is therefore to supplement direct communication rather than to replace it.

In the following two chapters, the design features are mapped to the service-oriented collaboration model. Table 3.5 provides an overview of the mapping between the design features and the model realizing them. How the design features for activities, participants, and composition are realized, is described in Chapter 4. The realization of participation and coordination is detailed in Chapter 5.

Table 3.5.: Mapping of design features to collaboration model.

Design Features	Realization in Collaboration Model
Activities and Participants	Component Model (Section 4.1)
Content Composition	Composition Model (Section 4.2)
Participation	Participation Protocol Framework (Section 5.1)
Coordination	Event Model (Section 5.2), Coordination Rule Mechanism (Section 5.3)

4. Component and Composition Model

Service composition serves as implementation technology for the design features described in Chapter 3. The nature of and assumptions on the elements to be composed in a service composition are captured in a component model [7, p. 256]. An assumption is for instance that all components are implemented using the same technologies. The *component model* presented in Section 4.1 assumes that elements to be composed expose a uniform interface regardless of being delivered by a human or software. A uniform interface potentially allows for the reduction of technical effort when replacing a participant, e.g., a Web service which is not available anymore, and the construction of collaboration systems which can automatically create and handle a large number of interfaces to services provided by humans.

In order to aggregate components into service-based applications, dependencies between components are defined using composition styles as outlined in Section 2.1.2. The *composition model* presented in Section 4.2 represents the aggregation of services which are delivered by human and non-human service providers in order to collaboratively create a document. Differently from the existing solutions, the composition can evolve during collaboration since the composition model allows coordinators to select and specify dependencies, providers, and services as required during execution of the composition. In addition, the use case of collaborative document creation is leveraged in order to enable coordination of the composition process itself: services aggregate contents into a document which is then used by coordinators to identify and specify new required activities.

4.1. Component Model

Services realize activities which are performed by participants of the collaboration. The component model describes the nature of services which can serve as basic building blocks of a service composition. Figure 4.2 presents a schematic overview of the component model, described using a UML class diagram.

Central to the component model is the *service* which represents a generic Web-accessible software entity able to perform an activity, more precisely, atomic content production activity as defined in design feature 1-3. A service might for instance provide statistical data, illustrate data as a diagram, send a document to a blog, or translate a text into another language. Each service possesses a serviceId which is a unique global identifier of a service. The optional serviceDescription carries an informal description of the activity that the service performs

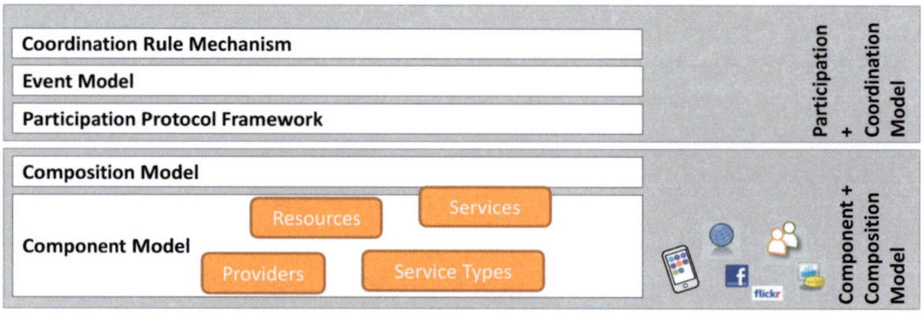

Figure 4.1.: Contribution "component model". In the component model the fundamental elements of a collaboration based on and targeted towards documents are identified. The objective of the component model is to provide a *uniform representation of human and non-human service providers* and their service types. Providers are potential participants of a collaboration offering resources and services.

written by the service provider. In order to address a service and request it, it provides a URI which denotes its physical location.

A service is associated with a number of *resources*. A resource is a container for any kind of content in an arbitrary format ranging from textual data to pictures or videos. In addition to content, a resource possesses a unique resourceId. In this thesis, a resource is understood as the output of a service rather than a requirement of a service to be able to execute, e.g., hardware resources. A resource might change over time.

A service manages the resources it possesses, i.e., provides them on request, updates, or deletes them. Each service exposes a uniform functional service interface for resource management. Calling the createOrUpdate() method on a service requests the creation of one or more new associated resources, or the update of existing ones. The delete() method requests the deletion of associated resources. Which resources are to be created, updated, or deleted is specified as parameter value of the methods.

The request() method allows service callers to retrieve the associated resource(s), e.g., to use them as parts in a collaboratively created document. Since services provided by humans might take time for their response to a request, the collaboration model provides an asynchronous communication protocol which is described in more detail in Section 5.1. A service might require input values in order to execute. For example, a search service requires a search string, or a human providing a text summary of a document requires the previous chapters of a document as input. A request might therefore come with an input parameter value or input parameter references to other services which can be requested by the service provider. The input is handled individually by services. For example, a service provided by humans might request all referenced services, store the requested resources locally, and present them on a graphical user interface (GUI) to the human provider.

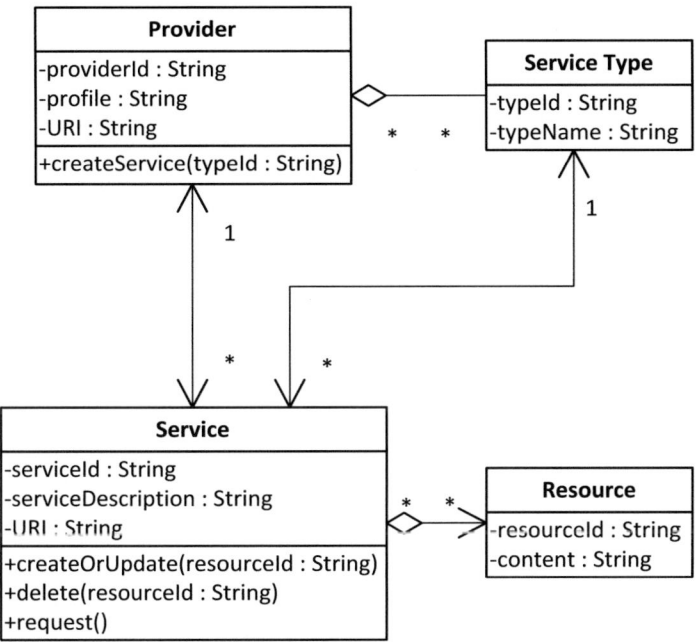

Figure 4.2.: Component model.

With each service, a *service type* is associated which characterizes the service in detail. Several services might exist with the same service type. A service type comes with a unique typeId and a typeName. Figure 4.3 presents an exemplary taxonomy of service types which captures activity types potentially performed during collaborative document creation.

A variety of service types for content provision, transformation, and publication exist which integrate human-based activities, automated mechanisms as well as external Web sources as defined in design feature 1-2. Content provision services, e.g., human-based authoring or content retrieval, provide existing or newly created contents which can be directly used in documents. Content transformation services, e.g., layout or language translation, produce content based on existing content which the retrieve as input resources. Publishing and approval services perform functional activities based on provided input resources. Such services might send content to external targets, e.g., e-mail addresses or Web servers.

Each service is offered by a *provider* which might, for instance, be a person, a Web information system, or an organization. A provider can offer several services of different service types. The required providerId is a unique identifier of a provider, the URI defines the address where a provider can be reached. An optional profile describes the skills and capabilities of a provider. A provider might offer service types without having associated concrete services

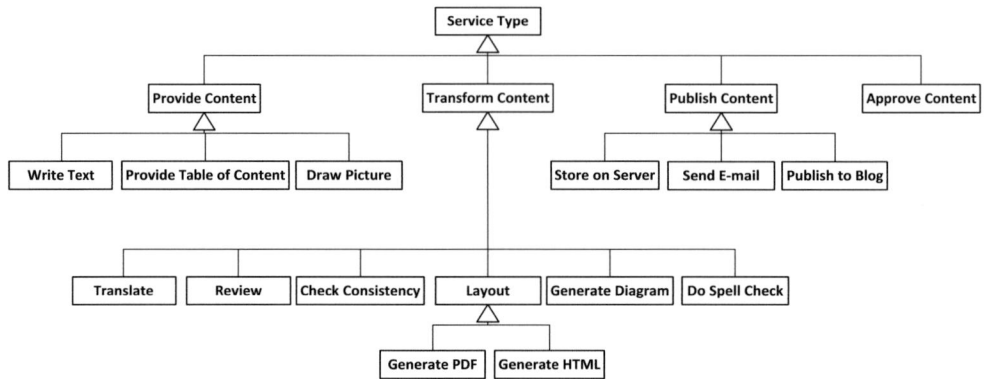

Figure 4.3.: Exemplary service type taxonomy for collaborative document creation.

of these types. The service types show the ability of a provider to perform certain tasks. Together with the profile, the information about associated service types can be used to match against requirements during a service selection procedure, e.g., during collaboration. The createService() method of a provider can be used to request the creation of a new service of a certain service type. This functionality is especially useful if a human is selected as provider but does not yet provide a concrete service.

Services as defined in the component model can be aggregated in order to produce a document composed of the resources they provide. The composition model presented in the following defines how services as well as resources are integrated in order to achieve a coherent document.

4.2. Composition Model

During collaboration, contributors perform activities to provide content to a joint document. These activities are represented as services as defined in the component model in the previous section. The composition model presented in the following defines how these services and their associated resources can be composed into an evolving document during collaboration. A simplified version of the composition model is described in [128]. A composition can be seen as both, activity composition and content composition, i.e., integrates activities performed by different participants as well as resources provided by the services. Figure 4.5 presents the composition model described in a UML class diagram.

The creation of a service composition according to the composition model is done by coordinators. Coordinators plan which content is expected, which activities, i.e., services, are required, as well as associate providers with certain activities. Providers performing

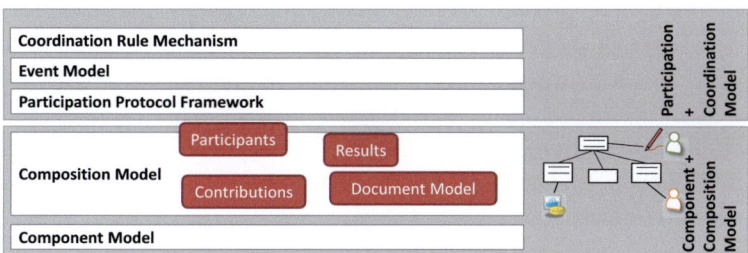

Figure 4.4.: Contribution "composition model". The composition model on top of the component model allows for the *representation of document evolution and refinement*. The composition model specifies how human coordinators can compose activities of participants (i.e., content provisioning and transformation) and delivered results into an evolving, hierarchical document. The objective is to provide a novel mechanism for end-users to flexibly compose resources and activities into one document.

associated services play contributor roles. The separation of coordinator and contributor roles is done according to design feature 1-1 to represent different capabilities and responsibilities of participants. A human can play both roles in a collaboration.

The goal of collaborative document creation is the creation of an electronic document for a particular purpose. A document can thus be considered the intended result of a collaboration. The composition model makes the *result* a first-class citizen of the collaboration. To start a service composition, one or more coordinators create a document structure representing the intended result structure and, in the course of collaboration, dynamically refine the structure through moving, adding, or deleting expected (sub)results. More precisely, they compose the document as an ordered tree of results which they expect or require to be delivered during collaboration. Concrete results could for instance be certain text sections. Each result has a unique resultId as well as exactly one parent (which is not itself) except the root result which has no parent result. Each result might contain an arbitrary number of subresults which can be added or removed during collaboration as required. The hierarchical structure might represent the logical structure of a document, e.g., if chapters and sections are associated with respective results. A hierarchical structure of a document prescribes the way how to interpret information presented in the document [52, p. 465]. A number of reference models for assembling documents exist, many of them structure their content components hierarchically. In addition, in most written documents and many multimedia presentations hierarchies of parts can be found [112][21]. The tree structure maps to other structures like flat or flow structures thus enables a range of document models.

A result is in a resultState. Which result states exist in a concrete composition depends on the collaboration application realized through the composition. Example states are "identified", "created", or "updated". Some applications might require an "approved" state denoting

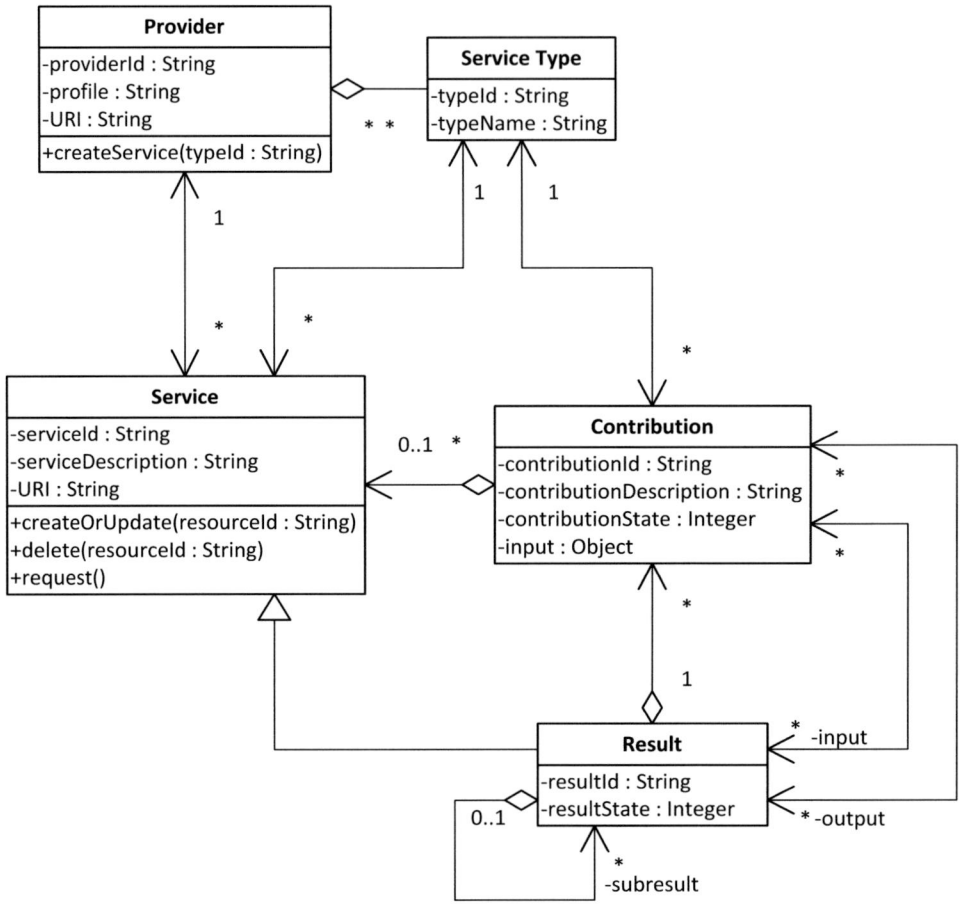

Figure 4.5.: Composition model.

a certain quality of the result. The result state is changed during collaboration through services or coordinators. More details on how the state might be changed during collaboration are provided in Section 5.1.

Results are services as defined in the component model denoted through the inheritance relationship shown in Figure 4.5. Therefore, results might possess a resource which contains content created and revised by contributors during collaboration. Results, however, can only possess one resource. Examples for content types are text, pictures, videos, footnotes, links/references, table of contents and other tables, or maps. The composition model therefore allows participants to create hierarchical documents which might contain any kind of content and does not prescribe a concrete document model as defined in design feature 2-2.

In order to access parts, i.e., results, of a document, clients access the request() method defined in the uniform interface of results. Documents or document parts can thus be reused in other documents as specified in design feature 2-3. Providers of these services are the coordinators of the results.

Having defined a number of expected results, coordinators identify *contributions* required to deliver and refine result content. A contribution is a placeholder for a concrete activity to be performed by a service during collaboration. Each result node might associate an arbitrary number of contributions, for instance, one for delivery of resource content and one for proofreading it. Placeholders for real services are useful, e.g., if at time of identification of a required activity no concrete service can be found yet. Contributions enable flexible selection and replacement of services during collaboration.

Contributions contain a unique contributionId as well as a contributionDescription of the activity to be performed. The description is accompanied with a service type and might be written by a coordinator to help participants carry out their activity. The contribution state captures state of the activity and helps coordinators to track state of the collaboration. Like the resultState, the contributionState depends on the concrete collaboration application. Example contribution states are "planned", "assigned", "idle", or "terminated". The state is changed during participation of a concrete service as described in more detail in Section 5.1.

As an example service composition, Figure 4.6 shows a snapshot of the project proposal document decomposed into chapters and sections associated with contributions to write, insert, proofread, or publish results.

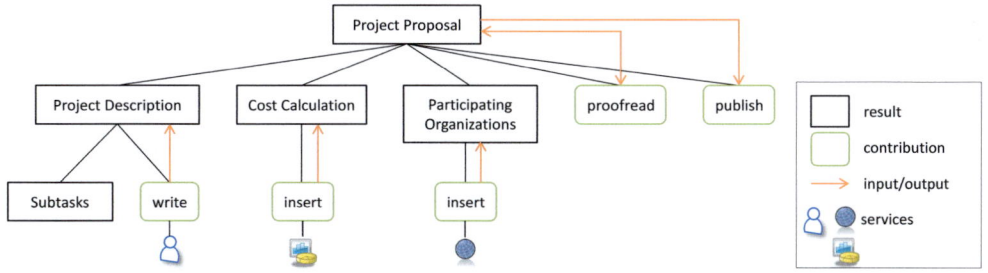

Figure 4.6.: Example composition of results and contributions with assigned services.

With each contribution, a concrete *service* might be associated which is responsible for providing an atomic activity related to the collaboration, i.e., produce new result content, or transform or publish existing result content. This service follows the component model as presented in the previous section. Providers of these services become contributors of the collaboration. Since services can be associated during composition execution, contributions enable late binding of services.

Coordinators might assign results as *input* to contributions. When calling the associated service, references to these input results are provided as parameter values for the requested service. The service can then request the content whenever needed through the request() method of the result. Sending references instead of contents allows associated services to retrieve content only when they need it. Content might be updated between a service request and a response. A service might check for content updates on its own. Alternatively or additionally to the input result references, a contribution might possess an input value which is sent to the service as parameter value of the request.

Which results are created or updated by the service associated with the contribution is specified by the coordinators through the *output* association of a contribution with a result. A service provides content via the update() method of the result which writes the content to the according resource(s). A service thus can deliver more than one result in a collaboration, for instance, writing a project description and drawing the project overview picture.

To summarize, coordinators perform several steps during creation of the service composition. Figure 4.7 provides an overview of the steps sorted into the phases followed by the classical service composition life cycle presented in Section 2.1.3.

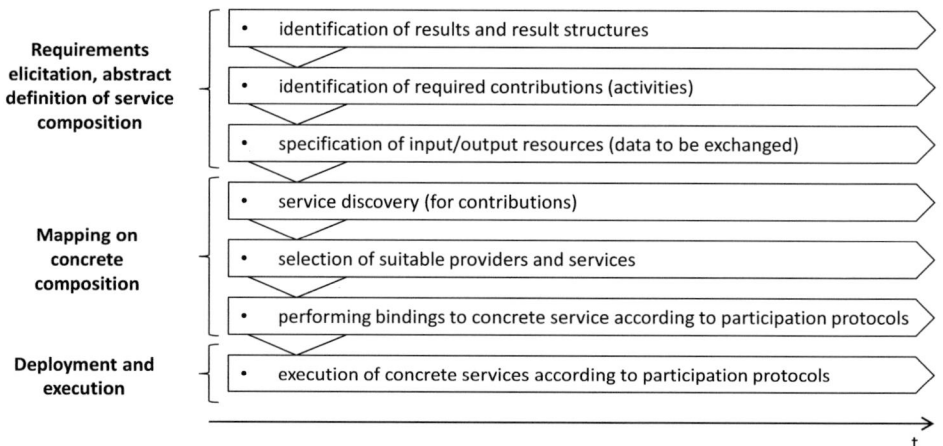

Figure 4.7.: Steps performed during service composition.

The steps performed during service composition do not follow a life cycle, rather each step can be performed as soon as minimum constraints are fulfilled. Coordinators start with identifying results and specifying an initial result structure. As soon as at least one result, e.g., the root result, is identified, coordinators can specify contributions which define the required activities. Required input and output results for these contributions can be specified now or at a later time during collaboration. Results and contributions can be added, moved, or removed anytime during collaboration which enables incremental structuring of evolving documents as required during collaboration and defined in design feature 2-1. The described steps are part of the requirements specification as well as abstract service composition definition.

As soon as a contribution is identified, mapping on concrete services can be started. This includes potentially the discovery of suitable service providers and services, the service selection as well as the service binding based on participation protocols as defined in Section 5.1. Services can be unbound or replaced with other services during collaboration. Service execution can start as soon as one concrete service is bound.

The life cycle of the service composition thus does not follow predefined phases. Rather, all specification steps can be performed during service composition execution which enables the flexibility of composition required for collaborative document creation.

4.3. Conclusion and Discussion

The component and composition model defined in the previous sections realize the design features specified in Chapter 3 as summarized in Table 4.1.

Table 4.1.: Realization of design features through component and composition models.

ID	Design Feature	Realization
DF 1-1	Support of coordinator and contributor roles.	Coordinators define service composition. Contributors are service providers delivering results.
DF 1-2	Integration of human and non-human participants providing data and functionality.	Service types provided by humans and non-humans are supported by the uniform service interface.
DF 1-3	Support for atomic content production activities.	Services manage resources which they can provide as contributions on request.
DF 2-1	Enable incremental structuring of documents and mapping of activities and content to structure.	Result tree capturing document structure can be modified throughout collaboration. Results are associated with contributions and activities.
DF 2-2	Independence of document model.	Each result resource in a document might have a different document model and format.
DF 2-3	Support reuse of produced content.	Results are services which provide document content on request.

The design decision for a *uniform service interface* in the component model has several implications for the application. On the one hand, a uniform interface restricts functionality of the services which are able to participate in a service composition. On the other hand, as all activities performed during collaboration are considered to be atomic, the simple interface suffices as it covers a large range of activities required in collaborative document creation. New services can be easily created without having to specify a detailed service description which potentially increases the number of available services.

The component model defines services as technology independent components. This enables the creation of adapters for existing services with different technologies, e.g. adapters to heterogeneous data sources or functionalities on the Web or in the enterprise. In addition, adapters with user interfaces for humans can be created which uniformly enable humans to manage the services they provide. Finally, plug-ins created for existing editors or adapters to other channels, e.g., e-mail, allow humans to provide their services using their existing or preferred tool environment. The development and reuse of adapters is simplified also through the uniform interface.

The specification of a uniform service interface for all services enables an easier replacement of services in a collaboration. Change to another service might be useful if persons providing services leave the team and an activity needs to be replaced, or Web services are not available anymore. In addition, the reusability of services is improved since the semantics for requesting activities are the same for all activities [142].

The composition model enables a new way of service composition. On the one hand, the document to be composed is a composition of *resources* which are exposed through service interfaces. The hierarchical grouping of resources into documents provides an intuitive but powerful model to the participants of collaborations as it enables coordination of collaboration through division of labor based on the document structure. The document model is inherently dynamic allowing the inclusion of functionality and contents of any format. On the other hand, the definition of contributions and association of services providing resources enables the composition of *activities*. The model therefore supports the fact that activities are distributed among team members and content is distributed over different sources. As described in Section 2.1.2, existing service composition styles often focus on either the execution of activities and the management of their dependencies or the composition of resources in a document.

The requirement of *flexibility* posed on the composition model by the case of collaborative document creation, is addressed through allowing specification of any part of the composition during execution. Due to the evolving nature of collaboration, the composition can not be completely specified in a dedicated design phase and instantiated in an execution phase. Rather, the composition continuously evolves during execution of a collaboration, i.e., results and contributions are added or removed, services are associated with contributions, and participants eventually execute services and deliver results. The collaboration manifests as the instantiation of the composition model. Existing artifact-centric approaches combining different composition styles require a model of the artifact before the composition can be executed and most often follow a certain data format.

The specification of complete models facilitates the *automated* execution of compositions [64]. Automation of compositions is desired, e.g., in order to automate business processes using workflow engines [3]. In flow-based styles, for example, the composed services should be automatically executed in the right order. The automated execution of compositions for collaborative document creation is difficult as the model continuously changes and evolves. In addition, the composition model does not allow for the specification of dependencies between activities. The specification and automation of such dependencies is supported by the coordination model introduced in the following chapter.

Several approaches exist which target automated service composition, e.g., based on semantic technologies (cf. [41]). The composition for collaborative document creation, however, is team and collaboration specific and the requirements of the participants might change throughout the collaboration. Coordinators identify and define requirements depending on the state of the collaboration, i.e., the contents produced, having the collaboration goal in mind. Automation mechanisms would have to understand state and goal of the collaboration. Complete automation therefore is difficult, if not impossible. Still, there is room for partial automation where the desired degree of automated composition depends on the use case. If, for example, participants want to create a number of documents with the same document structure, e.g., patterns in a pattern repository or bug fix descriptions, participants might wish to have a template mechanism at hand which automatically creates expected results as well as activities to create these results. In collaborations involving an open, unique document structure, automation might not be required or desired.

In the presented composition model, the human coordinator is the primary force driving the collaboration. The coordinator can distribute the required activities among participants. As soon as contributors are involved and services are executed, dependencies between activities or produced resources might occur which need to be coordinated. In the following chapter, the participation and coordination model is presented which (a) specifies protocols for the integration and execution of services and (b) addresses these coordination requirements.

5. Participation and Coordination Model

Human and non-human participants offer atomic activities of different types which are represented as services in the component model. Results produced or revised during service execution can be composed into a hierarchical, evolving document according to the composition model. In order to integrate services, coordinators need to communicate with them, e.g., ask human providers for commitment or request Web services to perform an activity. The integration of and communication with services or service providers follows well-defined *participation protocols*. As described in Section 3.3, the nature of required and supported protocols for participant integration and activity execution varies in different collaboration scenarios. In order to support different collaborative document creation use cases, Section 5.1 presents a *participation protocol framework* and an initial set of participation protocols. Within this framework, collaboration system providers can flexibly specify the protocols to be supported by their system. While existing coordination protocols and protocol frameworks, e.g., for WS-*, target non-human services the participation protocol framework enables the integration of human and non-human participants alike. Participation protocols can be automated as they are well-defined. Automation might be especially interesting for software services as they follow the same conversation sequence for each request.

While participation protocols support the coordination as regards the conversations between coordinators and providers, the *event model* (Section 5.2) and the *coordination rule mechanism* (Section 5.3) facilitate the automation of participation protocols as well as dependency management. For each associated service, participation protocols are executed which access document result elements, potentially in parallel. The execution of protocols might result in inconsistencies, e.g., if temporal or resource dependencies exist. Thus, each change of a state in a collaboration, e.g., during execution of a participation protocol, is denoted with an event. Specified rules might react on events and automatically perform activities. This automation reduces the manual effort of human coordinators during collaboration. In order to support a larger range of dependencies and protocols for different use cases, the event model and the rule mechanism can be configured and extended by collaboration system providers but also by coordinators of a collaboration.

5.1. Participation Protocol Framework

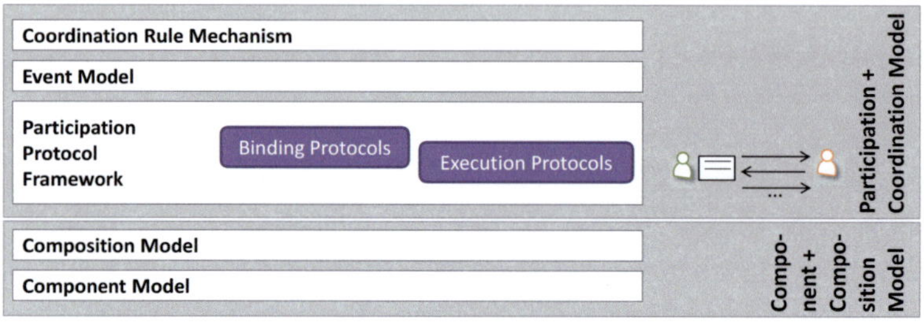

Figure 5.1.: Contribution "participation protocol framework". The participation protocol framework enables the definition of *participation protocols* for interactions between a coordinator and participants of a collaboration including service binding and service execution protocols. The objective of the participation protocol framework is to enable the flexible selection of protocols according to the use case requirements. A set of protocols is presented which support different collaboration scenarios.

Participation protocols define conversation sequences during interactions of coordinators and providers or services. For instance, a human provider and a coordinator communicate in order to agree on the contribution the provider performs in the collaboration. In project teams it might be common practice for a project coordinator to delegate tasks to team members who have to perform them. In other teams, participants might first negotiate or be free to decline an assigned task. The inclusion of human and software service providers at the same time requires the technical support of participation protocols which can be handled by both types of service providers.

The activity to be performed is the context of this interaction between coordinator and provider or service. The participation protocols define valid states of an activity and state transitions of the activity in a collaboration. In the collaboration model, an activity is manifested through the contribution element of the composition model. A contribution maintains the state of the activity in the contributionState field. Participants of a collaboration, i.e., coordinators or providers, are able to access the contribution state or change it according to the participation protocols.

Figure 5.2 shows a schematic overview of the main states in the life cycle of a contribution. As soon as a participant identifies the need for a contribution, he creates a contribution element, for instance, to proofread the project proposal. Eventually, a service needs to be *bound* to the collaboration which ensures the provider's commitment to contribute a certain service for the collaboration as well as the consent of the coordinator. For instance, a person is asked if he is willing to proofread the project proposal collaboration. If the person accepts, the

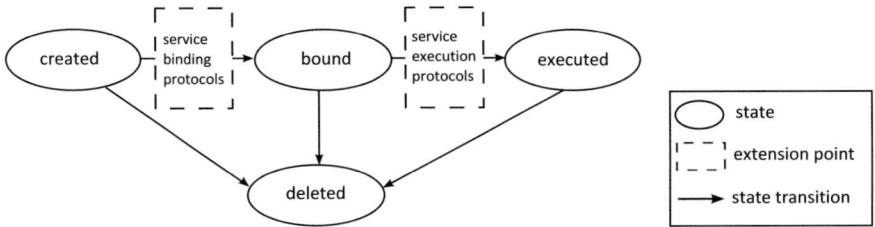

Figure 5.2.: Overview of participation protocols in contribution life cycle.

proofreading service he provides is bound to the proofreading contribution. Such protocols for binding of a service to a contribution are called *binding protocols*.

In Web services, the activity of binding is also called service selection. Service selection specifies how and when a concrete service is bound to a composition [7, p. 267ff.]. In static binding, the endpoint of a service is specified directly in the composition. Dynamic binding, where the endpoint of the service is looked up at a directory or calculated based on a specified query just before execution, eases replacement of services. Service selection looks at binding procedures from the composition's viewpoint, which is the viewpoint of the coordinator in the case of collaborative document creation. The binding of services provided by humans, however, also involves interactions of the coordinator with the service providers and thus requires adoption of binding protocols, e.g., for negotiation.

From the state "bound", a contribution can transfer to state "executed". This is performed through *execution protocols*, i.e., the bound service is *requested* to be performed. As an example, the coordinator decides that the project proposal is ready to be proofread and calls the service associated with the according contribution. In this case, the person delivers the results asynchronously. In case a software service is involved, the response to the service call might be synchronous. During all stages, a contribution can be deleted, e.g., if it is not required anymore.

The dashed boxes in Figure 5.2 are placeholders for participation protocols which are implemented in concrete collaboration systems in order to ensure correct state transfers of contributions during communication. These boxes are extension points in the collaboration model. In the following, a set of basic participation protocols are proposed which enable the participation of providers and their services in a collaboration. Earlier versions of the participation protocols are described in [128].

The basic participation protocols are described using a slightly modified version of the diagram type used in the WS-Coordination protocols WS-BA [98] and WS-AT [94] and described as coordination protocol graph (CPG) in [72]. The nodes of this directed graph are states, the edges denote messages which are exchanged by the participating entities which lead to state transitions of the communicating parties. Messages can originate from different parties which is denoted by dashed and solid lines. The diagram type is chosen as it allows for the graphical representation of messages from different participants and the effects of those messages on a state in one diagram. The following protocol snippets are part of the overall contribution life cycle and therefore do not present an explicit starting or ending node. As opposed to the CPG, the protocol flow might contain cycles, e.g., it might return to the state "created". In addition, a (human) coordinator might want to decide which step in the protocol to take next. Therefore, more than one outgoing edge with the same participant is allowed for a node.

5.1.1. Service Binding Protocols

Service binding is the association of a service to a contribution. Service binding can be initiated by coordinators or service providers which implies different protocols, namely (a) coordinator-initiated service binding and (b) self-service binding of a provider.

(a) *Coordinator-initiated service binding protocol.* A coordinator might choose a provider suitable for a contribution in his collaboration and ask the provider to participate. Figure 5.3 shows this coordinator-initiated service binding protocol. Having created a contribution, the coordinator associates the contribution with a provider, where the contribution state is "binding open". According to the protocol, the coordinator then asks a provider for binding a service which changes the contribution state to "asked for binding". The binding request can be aborted by the coordinator, which transfers the contribution back to the state "binding open". A service provider might decline or accept the binding request. A contribution is then "bound" with the service. In case the binding is not required anymore or another service should be bound, the binding can be completely deleted by the coordinator. Variations of the protocol might exist, e.g., that deleting a binding is also allowed for the provider.

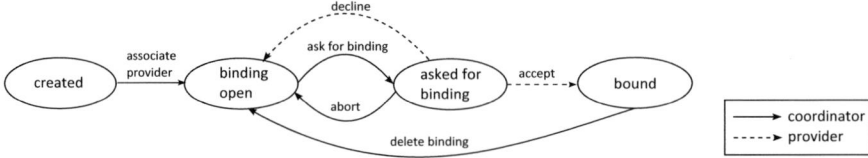

Figure 5.3.: Coordinator-initiated binding protocol.

(b) *Self-service binding protocol.* A provider might volunteer for a contribution and apply for it following a self-service binding protocol. In this case, the coordinator has to decide whether to accept the application as shown in Figure 5.4. Self-service binding might be useful in human collaboration where for instance participants discussed and allocated activities verbally.

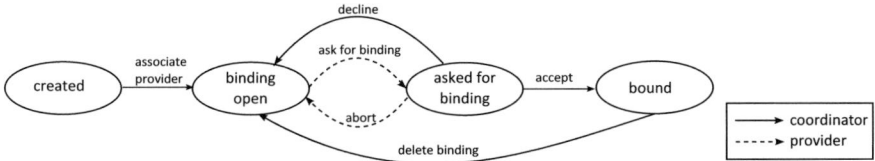

Figure 5.4.: Self-service binding protocol.

If both protocols are to be implemented in a single collaboration system, the contribution needs to store additional state information, e.g., whether provider or coordinator already accepted a binding request. More complex binding protocols could involve resource allocation or negotiation mechanisms, e.g., to choose the best or best available service or negotiate additional conditions. Especially for services provided in the enterprise, authorization protocols might be useful.

5.1.2. Service Execution Protocols

Once bound, a service can be requested and eventually deliver, transform, publish, or approve result content. In the following a set of protocols is described regulating the service execution communication: (a) The service request-response protocol defines how performing a contribution influences a result. (b) The service request-response protocol can be extended with approval. (c) The input retrieval protocol allows service providers to retrieve the existing result contents which is declared as input to the contribution.

(a) *Service request-response protocol.* The execution of a service influences the state of the results it has to deliver or refine. The result state is captured in the resultState attribute in result element of the composition model. Which results a service has to work on, is specified in the composition model through the output association of a contribution to results. A contribution might thus deliver several results in one execution or execute several times in order to provide all results its contribution is associated with. For instance, one person might be responsible for providing texts for the main part of the project proposal which is split into several results. The according contribution is associated with all of those results through the output association. The person, however, can deliver one result after the other through providing its service several times.

Figure 5.5(a) shows the life cycle of a contribution which influences the life cycle of a result. The corresponding result life cycle is shown in Figure 5.5(b). The dotted arrows denote influences of the execution of service A on the result life cycle. Another service B might also influence the result. The life cycle of service B is not shown in the figures.

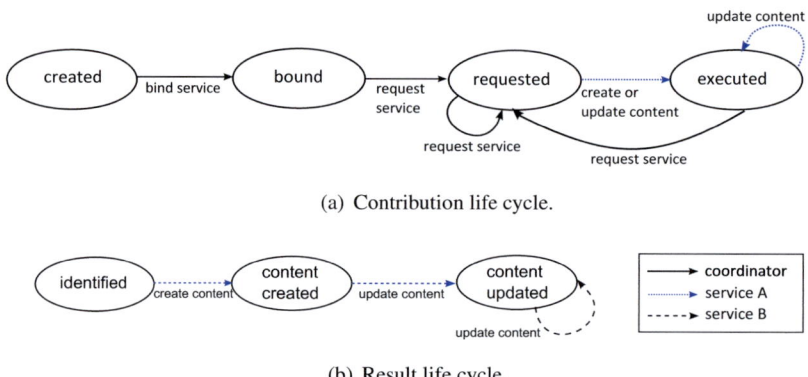

(a) Contribution life cycle.

(b) Result life cycle.

Figure 5.5.: Service request-response protocol.

As soon as a contribution is bound with a service, service A in the example, a coordinator might request the execution of the service by calling its request() method. The contribution which captures the protocol state for the service is transferred to state "requested". The contribution can be requested again, e.g., if the contributor does not react until a specified point in time. Being requested, a service provider eventually produces contents and contributes it to the corresponding result. The result turns to state "content created" or "content updated" if content was already created, e.g., through another contribution. In state "executed" the contribution can be called again through the coordinator or executed again through the service provider, e.g., for updates of a text. A repeated request can be used as a reminder for human services. Publishing activities do not have an impact on the result life cycle.

As an example, a service bound to a contribution is requested to deliver the project description. As soon as the service provider creates the content, i.e., the project description, the result changes to state "created". The "update content" activity of a service might update one to all output result contents of the contribution associated with the service.

The service request-response protocol allows for the decoupling of request and response. A service might provide several logically coupled results by responding to one service call, e.g., writing the abstract and the summary of a document. Furthermore, provider respond synchronously (for software services) or asynchronously (for human services).

(b) *Service request-response protocol with approval.* The approval of a result or the declaration of a contribution to be finished might be important to ensure quality, e.g., through the four-eyes principle. Special approval service types are used in the following to realize approval protocols. The service request-response protocols are extended with additional states. Figure 5.6(b) shows a result whose content is originally created by a service A. Figure 5.6(a) presents the contribution life cycle of the approval service B responsible for approving the result.

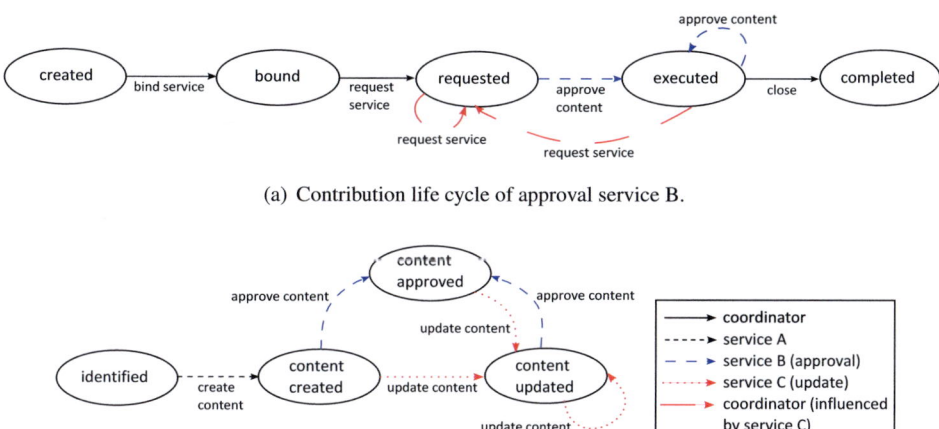

(a) Contribution life cycle of approval service B.

(b) Result life cycle.

Figure 5.6.: Service request-response protocol with approval.

Accordingly, the execution of the approval service B triggers the transfer of the corresponding result to state "content approved". As soon as another service, e.g., service C in the figure, updates the approved result, approval service B is called again by the coordinator as denoted by the red arrows. Optionally, a contribution might be closed by a coordinator when it is not required anymore or the coordination considers it to be finished.

(c) *Input Retrieval Protocol.* Services might need to retrieve input like parts of the result content which already exists. For instance, a translation service needs as input the text it has to translate. A human translator might also require additional context information, e.g., already translated content, in order to produce high quality content. Input might also contain configuration parameters for a service, e.g., keywords or values. Reading the input means navigating through the result tree. Each request to an input result returns the content of the resource associated with this result as well as URIs to other results associated with this result (e.g., subresults) which can also be requested by the provider. This way, the service can retrieve as many input results as required. The input might be read during any state of the contribution life cycle. Access control mechanisms like authorization protocols or role models might be implemented on top.

The input retrieval protocol is inspired by the HATEOAS principle of REST[47, p. 82], although no application state is changed in the first place. Service providers can decide which result contents they would like to retrieve. They can execute the protocol at any time. Transferring content in a parameter value at the time of the service request could possibly result in a service working on outdated data. The provider also does not need to store result content, e.g., if he decides to work on the contribution at a later point in time. The provider just needs to know one result URI which is provided through the input relationship associated with the contribution. The document structure is not need to be known. The protocol thus works with flat or hierarchical models.

5.1.3. Conclusion and Discussion

The participation protocol framework realizes the design features specified in Chapter 3 as shown in Table 5.1.

Table 5.1.: Realization of design features through participation protocol framework.

ID	Design Feature	Realization
DF 3-1	Support different protocols for finding contributors and associating them to activities.	Participation protocol framework allows for integration of different use case specific service binding protocols.
DF 3-2	Associate execution of activities with document part states.	Execution protocols manage association between contribution state and result state.
DF 3-3	Enable participants to access (parts of) the document and use it as input.	Results are services which can be accessed through requesting them using an input retrieval protocol.

The participation protocol framework is a simple framework for the integration of service providers into a collaboration. Depending on the use case to be supported by a specific collaboration system, suitable protocols are selected or defined for the system and implemented, e.g., using a protocol engine. All participants in a collaboration need to support the specified participation protocols. Besides the described example protocols, collaboration systems could implement sophisticated authentication protocols or protocols for pushing result contents to participating providers.

Unifying the protocols in a collaboration eases the integration of new participants which is required in collaborative document creation where the contributions and participants can not be specified in advance. The specification of protocols allows collaboration systems to (semi-)automate protocol execution depending on the use case or participant. For example, services might automatically be requested when they change to state "bound". Software services might themselves perform automated execution, e.g., automatically accept requests for bindings or decline them in case they are overloaded. Automation of protocols is described in the following sections.

As described in Chapter 4, flexible participation is realized through the fact that specification can be performed during execution of the service composition. The conversations can therefore be started at any time during collaboration. The collaboration is started as soon as the first result node is created. The document itself is seen to be constantly evolving during collaboration. Thus, the shown protocols do not include a "finish" state of a result. Still, collaboration system designers might specify protocols for the protocol framework which involve such a state for a result.

The participation protocol framework is inspired by the WS-Coordination framework [96]. The main difference between the frameworks is the interactions they focus. Besides simple interactions, WS-Coordination protocols potentially support long-running transactions, mainly focused on non-human participants. The protocols might involve several participants. Participation protocols as presented in the previous sections are restricted to coordinating interactions between two participants for the goal of service binding or service execution. The participation protocols allow coordinators to integrate humans and software services alike. Complex interactions between several participants, however, are not considered in the current version of the framework. The participation protocols, however, are lightweight because no complex, long-running conversations are required in order to bind a service or provide a result. As no specific logic is required for deciding the next steps, the implementation of the protocols should be straight-forward.

WS-Coordination provides a *context* for communication which is created through a dedicated activation service on request of one participant. In the participation protocol framework, the contribution element builds the context for the definition of protocols for allocating and requesting participants as well as executing work. In WS-Coordination, the context is exchanged between participants through messages. In contrary, in the participation protocol framework, a shared data approach is applied where all participants can access the contribution. Contributions are resources which capture the state of conversations. Participants do not have to store state information of a conversation. As the contribution captures the state of a conversation centrally as a resource, services themselves can be stateless. This potentially allows for better reusability (e.g., higher level services like "writing" can be offered instead of "writing abstract for project proposal X"). Service providers, however, have to be able to observe the contributions they are responsible for. Coordinators are enabled to access and track conversation state of all contributions in a collaboration. State tracking is a coordination mechanism which can be applied for collaborative document creation to track progress of a collaboration.

In WS-Coordination, a registration service allows a Web service to register for a specific activity in a specific context using a particular coordination protocol. A Web service may engage for a number of activities at the same time. Similarly, in the participation protocol framework, providers might also participate in a number of activities for binding and executing services. Registration for a specific activity therefore is similar to binding a service to a contribution. The binding in the participation protocol framework might follow different protocols.

Participation protocols technically enable providers to be bound and to contribute to a collaboration. In a collaboration, a large range of conversations happen, potentially at the same time. These conversations might depend on each other or influence the same results. Coordination mechanisms enable the management of dependencies. During state changes of contributions and results, events are emitted which can be used for these coordination mechanisms, e.g., to reduce manual coordination efforts for the coordinator. The following section presents the event model.

5.2. Event Model

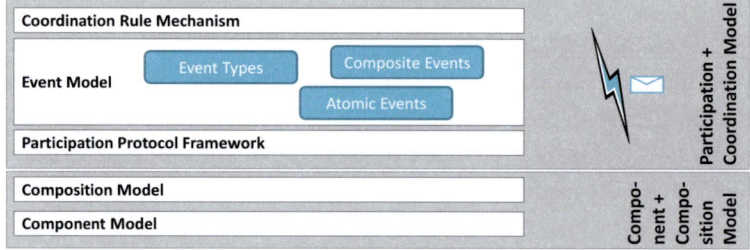

Figure 5.7.: Contribution "event model". The event model *defines atomic and composite events* which might occur during collaboration, i.e., changes of the service composition and execution of participation protocols. The event model is extensible in order to be adaptable to a range of use cases.

Activities in a collaboration might be of interest for other participants in a collaboration. For instance, a coordinator might want to track the state of a collaboration through monitoring which contributions are provided and which are open. A coordinator might want to send reminders to services of open contributions, e.g., to manage deadline dependencies. Coordination should be automated in order to reduce manual coordination efforts. As a basis for automation serves an *event* mechanism based on the participation protocols presented in the previous section as well as the activities performed by coordinators during composition of results and contributions as described in Section 4.2.

An event is "anything that happens, or is contemplated as happening" [82]. An event refers to the change of a state of a real or virtual object or attribute of an object [19, p. 48]. Types of events range from physical or technical events occurring with a high frequency to business or human-triggered events [19, p. 85f.]. Figure 5.8 presents the structure of *atomic event types* in the collaboration model. An extract of the structure is published in [128]. Instances of the event types are emitted during collaboration, e.g., caused by coordination activities which change state of service bindings or service response activities. Each state change in the participation protocols triggers an event.

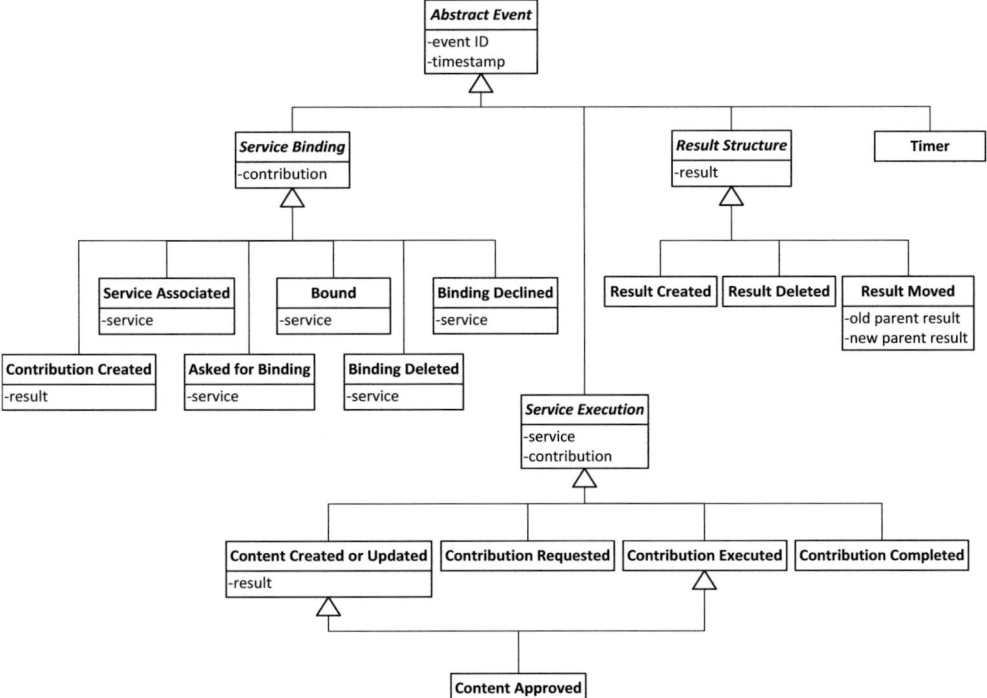

Figure 5.8.: Atomic event types for collaborative document creation.

The model follows established techniques for event definition (cf. [19]). Accordingly, each event type inherits from an abstract event type and includes a unique ID and a timestamp denoting the time of emission. In addition, each event exposes context-specific information like its source or the result which was changed. Events of the type *service binding* are emitted during the service binding protocols presented in the previous section. Events of the type *service execution* capture all events of the result and contribution life cycles during execution of a service. Changes on the overall result tree structure, e.g., creating or moving results, are denoted by events of the type *result structure*. Events of the type *timer* are emitted at specified points in time. New event types can be added by collaboration system designers as required through inheriting *abstract event*. Adding new event types might be required if additional participation protocols are implemented defining new states and transitions.

In addition to atomic events, *derived* or *composite* events [82] might be captured during collaboration. Derived events are events which are generated by a method based on the occurrence or non-occurrence of other events. For instance, an event might be triggered if a certain contribution was not executed until a certain point in time. The event is derived from the *absence* of an event.

Composite events mark a more complex situation and are derived events which connect atomic events. During collaborations, event streams of atomic events are produced which are continuously queried by event processing engines in order to detect *event patterns* [19, p. 18ff.] representing complex situations. A number of event specification languages exist to define event patterns. For example, event patterns can be defined using event algebras, also called composition-operator-based languages [43, p. 49ff.], which specify dependencies and constraints for a set of events [19, p. 109]. Dependencies like sequences are defined using operators over event types or event data. Alternative languages are, for example, data stream query and production rule languages (cf. [43, p. 56ff.] for a detailed discussion).

Event patterns in the collaboration model are specified using an event algebra since such languages are perceived to be intuitive and easy to use for developers [43, p. 69]. The language, which is inspired by [19, p. 110f.], supports only few operators in order to minimize potential misinterpretations and misunderstandings of patterns by collaboration participants. An early version of the language is published in [128]. The language is designed to provide an initial mechanism to detect complex situations in collaborative document creation rather than to be all-embracing and formally correct. Sufficiency and usability of the specified mechanism needs to be evaluated in collaboration scenarios in future work.

Event pattern specification is based on the operators conjunction, disjunction, sequence, and negation which are supported by all existing composition-operator-based languages [43, p. 51]:

- A $\wedge$ B defines a *conjunction* which denotes that both, an event of type A and an event of type B, have to occur in order to fulfill the event pattern regardless of the order of their occurrence.

- A $\vee$ B defines a *disjunction* which denotes that either an event of type A or an event of type B has to occur in order to fulfill the event pattern.

- A $\rightarrow$ B defines a *sequence* which denotes that the pattern is detected if an event of type A is followed by an event of type B.

- $\neg$ A defines a *negation* which denotes the non-occurrence of an event of type A during a specified time window. The absence of an event might denote a potential inconsistency, e.g., if an update of a diagram was denoted by an event but not the update of the describing text.

In addition, conditions on the attribute values of an event type might be specified. For example, A(id–"123") describes an event pattern for an event of type A with the ID 123. In the following, such event types are called conditioned.

Operators can be combined to construct more complex event patterns. For example, the pattern A $\rightarrow$ (B $\vee$ C) describes an event pattern where an event of type A is followed by either an event of type B or of type C [19, p. 110]. Events of type timer can be specified in an event pattern using the template Timer(year-month-day-hour-minute). For example, the event Timer(2013-06-01-8-30) is detected on June 1st, 2013 at 8.30am. The event Timer(*-*-*-14-00) is detected every day at 2pm.

Additionally, the following assumptions are made for the event model.

- An event stream comprises all events of exactly one collaboration. Events in an event stream are ordered based on their time of occurrence.

- If two event types are connected with an operator, e.g., A $\wedge$ B, any event of arbitrary type might occur in between the events of type A and type B, unless otherwise specified through a negation, e.g., A $\wedge$ B $\wedge \neg$ C.

- If an event pattern contains a negation, the pattern implicitly defines a time window in which the negation holds. The time window starts when the first event matching the pattern is detected, and ends when the last required event or an event of the negated event type is detected. For example, for the event pattern A $\rightarrow$ (B $\wedge \neg$ C) the time window starts as soon as an event of type A is detected and expires as soon as an event of type B is detected denoting the successful derivation of the composite event.

Atomic and composite events denote situations in a collaboration which are made explicit through the extensible event model. As defined in design feature 4-1, events support basic coordination as they can be seen as a notification on a situation which might require action from a coordinator or provider. More sophisticated coordination means can be based on events in form of rules. The coordination rule mechanism is presented in the following section.

5.3. Coordination Rule Mechanism

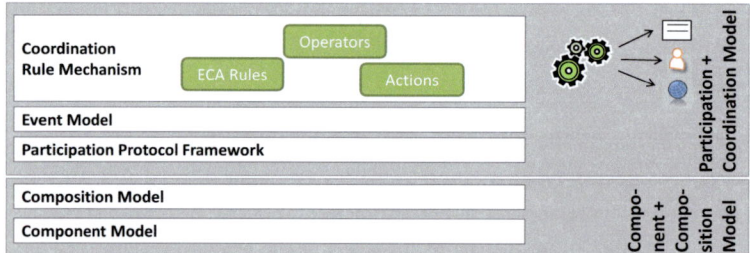

Figure 5.9.: Contribution "coordination rule mechanism". An *ECA rule mechanism* enables participants to specify rules reacting on events. Rules allow for coordination of collaborations, including the partial automation of participation protocols and the management of dependencies between activities and results. Frequent dependencies between activities are identified and rules are proposed to manage them.

The service composition supported by the component and composition model defined in Chapter 4 as well as the participation protocols enable manual execution of a service composition supporting collaboration. The specification and execution of the service composition is mainly driven by the coordinators of a collaboration. The coordination rule mechanism described in this section enables, on the one hand, the reduction of manual coordination effort through (semi-)automation. On the other hand, the mechanism supports additional coordination means based on events occurring during collaboration.

Figure 5.10 depicts potential dependencies occurring during collaborative creation of a project proposal which might need to be coordinated. Several persons provide input to the project description which poses a shared resource dependency on the result. A content dependency exists between the project description and the project overview picture. Once the project description is updated, the project description has to be aligned. In the example, a Web service inserts the profile descriptions of the participating organizations. A translation activity performed on these descriptions requires them as input which denotes a producer/-

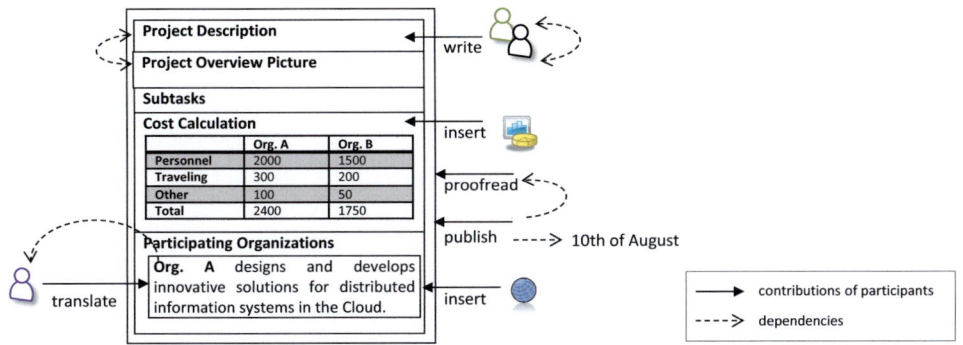

Figure 5.10.: Dependencies during collaborative creation of a project proposal document.

consumer relation between the activities. Finally, the document should not be published before it is proofread – a prerequisite relation.

In order to manage such dependencies, coordinators can specify coordination rules which are handled by a coordination rule engine. A rule consists of a set of events as defined in the previous section, a set of conditions, and a set of actions. The set of conditions might be empty. At least one event and one action are required.

- *Event* patterns are specified as presented in Section 5.2. If an event pattern matches, i.e., an atomic or composite event occurs, the rule is activated, conditions are checked, and actions are executed.

- *Conditions* are functions over events, event attributes, and environment variables. A function might check whether an attribute conforms to a specific value, e.g., whether the event occurred in a specific time interval or the event refers to a certain result. In addition, conditions might be arbitrary functions performing calculations or checking attribute values. The return value of the functions are either "true" or "false". A condition might be composed of a set of conditions which are concatenated through conjunctions or disjunctions. If the condition is evaluated to true, actions are executed according to the rule specification.

- *Actions* are automated activities triggered by a rule. Actions either emit derived events or they call services according to the participation protocols.

Only one event can occur at a time. Events are placed into a queue which is processed by the rule engine on a first in first out basis. The rule engine is push-based, i.e., whenever an event occurs all rules are selected which match this event. Potentially, not all events in an event pattern are fulfilled. Rules with partially fulfilled event patterns are annotated with a note and a timestamp that the event was already detected. Rules in which the event pattern is completed are checked for their conditions. If the condition returns false, nothing happens. If the condition returns true or no condition exists, all actions of the rule are executed. The event is deleted from the queue.

During execution of rules, several conflicts or inconsistencies might occur. Loops might omit termination, e.g., if events triggering a rule are also emitted in the action part of the rule. General possible resolution mechanisms for loops include static analysis of rules before execution as well as restricting the cascading level of rules [30].

A pragmatic resolution mechanism is to forbid the creation of rules which listen to the same event as emitted in the action. Another example conflict is a loop which occurs if an update of a service triggers the update of another service, which again triggers an update of the first service. Such loops might be required, e.g., if two interdependent results should be kept up to date. The scenario can be avoided if human services and coordinators are involved which can control the execution of the rule. As soon as both services are automated software services, however, the rule might cause problems.

Different execution orders of rules might result in different states of results or contributions. For instance, two rules listen to the same event and both rules change the state of the same contribution, one to "bound" the other to "binding open". In order to avoid such conflicts, a static analysis approach could be applied which checks rules at their creation in order to avoid conflicts with already existing rules. Alternatively, the creator of rules might prioritize rules [30]. The usability of rule prioritization for end-users as the intended target group of the collaboration model, however, has to be examined.

Analysis of rule bases and mechanisms to ensure termination as well as avoid conflicts caused by the execution order, i.e., ensure confluence, is and has been subject to research, especially in the active database domain [106]. Evaluation of applicability of existing approaches or design of new mechanisms is out of scope in this thesis.

Rules are specified by coordinators over the event types as described in Listing 5.1 using the Extended Backus-Naur Form (EBNF) [61].

```
(* Specification of rule: *)
rule = ' ON ', event, [' IF ', condition], ' DO ', action ;

(* Specification of event pattern according to the event model: *)
event = [¬] atomic-event | [¬] conditioned-event
            | [¬] composite-event ;
atomic-event = ? atomic event type ? ;
conditioned-event = atomic-event, (, ? event attribute ?, =,
            '"', ? value ? ,'"', ) ;
composite-event = [(], event, operator, event, [)] ;
```

```
operator = → | ∧ | ∨ ;


(* Specification of conditions: *)
condition = simple-condition | composed-condition ;
composed-condition = [(], condition, (' AND '|' OR '),
           condition, [)] ;
simple-condition = atomic-event, '.', ? event attribute ? ,
                   (=|!=|>|<|=>|=< , '"', ? value ? , '"'
           | '[', timestamp,',', timestamp, ']'
           | ? function with parameters ? ;


(* Specification of actions: *)
action = simple-condition | composed-condition ;
simple-action = ? function with parameters ? ;
composed-action = action, ' AND ', action ;
```

Listing 5.1: Rule language specified in EBNF.

As described in the event model in the previous section, an event pattern can either contain a single atomic event or a composite event. Both, an atomic or a composite event can be negated using the symbol ¬. An `atomic-event` is of an atomic event type as specified in the event model. For the specification of a `composite-event`, the `operator` symbols defined in the previous section for concatenating events can be used: → for sequence, ∧ for conjunction, and ∨ for disjunction. The optional `condition` might be simple composed. A `simple-condition` contains one function. A `composed-condition` concatenates several conditions using the operators `AND` for conjunction or `OR` for disjunction. In a `condition`, event attributes can be used for filtering using the dot operator, e.g., to listen for bound events concerning a particular contribution. The expression operators =, !=, >, <, =>, =< can be used for comparing an attribute to a value. For instance, e1.id="123" matches if the ID attribute of the e1 event has the value "123". A condition might also call a function with specific parameters which evaluates to true or false. A condition might specify a time frame in which the event pattern has to be fulfilled using a start and an end `timestamp`. A rule might trigger one or more actions. The `simple-action` specifies a function to be called, for instance, a request to a particular service. A `composed-action` composes two or more simple actions using the `AND` operator.

Rules are either generic or collaboration-specific. Generic rules apply for all collaborations of the same type which can be supported by the same collaboration system. Collaboration-specific rules support coordination of one collaboration and are defined by the coordinator(s) of this collaboration. A collaboration system employs a mixture of generic and collaboration-specific rules. The required rules differ for each use case and potentially for each single collaboration. Features supported by rules are (a) the (semi-)automated execution of participation protocols mainly supported by generic rules, (b) the specification and coordination of collaboration-specific dependencies, and (c) the detection and management of potential inconsistencies through suggesting or generating rules. In the following, an exemplary set of rules is presented for these features.

5.3.1. Rules for Semi-Automation of Participation Protocols

The participation protocols presented in Section 5.1 prescribe steps to be followed for binding and invoking a service. In order to support a human coordinator in execution of these steps, service binding and invocation can be performed automatically by a coordination engine implemented in a collaboration system. A semi-automation, i.e., the automation of a subset of the steps required to complete a protocol execution, can be reached through configuring the coordination engine with the following rules (adapted version of the automation rule specified in [128]).

```
ON ServiceAssociated
DO askForBinding(ServiceAssociated.contribution)
ON Bound
DO requestContribution(Bound.contribution)
```

These rules are triggered as soon as an event of type `ServiceAssociated` or `Bound` is detected. An event of type `ServiceAssociated` is emitted whenever a coordinator adds a service to a contribution. The first rule is activated and subsequently the rule engine calls as action the `askForBinding` method which sends a message to the associated service asking it for acceptance of the binding according to the service binding protocol. As soon as a binding is accepted, i.e., an event of type `Bound` is detected, the second rule calls the `requestContribution` method. This method calls the associated service.

A human coordinator can restrict this behavior through extending the rules, e.g., if a specific service should not be called automatically. The following rule prevents the execution of the action if the bound service has the ID `publish`. The specified rule becomes collaboration-specific.

```
ON Bound
IF Bound.service!="publish"
DO requestContribution(Bound.contribution)
```

5.3.2. Rules for Coordinating Collaboration-Specific Dependencies

A second use case for coordination rules is the management of collaboration-specific dependencies. This section provides a set of rules which can be built with the rule mechanism and might be useful during collaboration as explained in Section 3.4.

As introduced in Section 2.3, *prerequisite relations*, i.e., the requirement that one activity can only be performed when another activity is finished, or *producer/consumer relations*, i.e., that one activity creates input for another activity, might occur. Such dependencies can be handled through task sequencing or notifications. The following rule reacts on the creation or update of a specific result – the result with ID `project description` – in order to request the contribution with ID `translate`.

```
ON ContentCreatedOrUpdated(result="project description")
DO requestContribution("translate")
```

The rule can also help to manage *content dependencies* where two results interrelate. These rules are specific to the collaboration and have to be created for each dependency if coordination of the dependency is desired. Fully automating such dependencies is difficult as they require an understanding of the content of the artifact. The combination of the sequencing rule with rule-based automated service requests in one collaboration could cause a request to the translate service before potential result content for the project description is provided.

In order to manage *temporal dependencies* in a restricting way, i.e., disallow the execution of particular actions, a collaboration system could decouple the intent to request a service from the actual request [128]. Events of type `ContributionRequested` could be interpreted as the intention to request the contribution. An event of type `ContributionRequested` is emitted as soon as the coordinator requests a contribution, but before the call is sent to the associated service. The rule engine can then be configured with rules constraining the request of specific services unless particular events have occurred.

At each occurrence of an event of type `ContributionRequested`, the following rule requests the service specified in the event (adapted version from the rule presented in [128]).

```
ON ContributionRequested
DO requestService(ContributionRequested.service)
```

In order to introduce restrictions, the rule can be extended with conditions, for instance, if a prerequisite relationship holds, e.g., the publish service should only be performed after the proofread was done. As extension, the coordinator adds a condition to the rule which prevents the execution of the service call to the publish service and a rule which only executes the service if the proofread already updated some content:

```
ON ContributionRequested
IF ContributionRequested.service!="publish"
DO requestService(ContributionRequested.service)

ON ContributionRequested(service="publish") ∧
      ContentCreatedOrUpdated(service="proofread")
DO requestService(ContributionRequested.service)
```

The rule mechanism enables the specification of reminders in order to improve management of *deadline dependencies*. For instance, if the result with ID cost calculation section in the project proposal is not created or updated until February, 18th in 2013, the contribution with the ID cost calculation is requested. The rule does not ensure deadline accordance, however, the coordinator is free in defining times for reminders.

```
ON Timer(2013-02-18-00-00) ∧
      ¬ ContentCreatedOrUpdated(result="cost calculation section")
DO requestContribution("cost calculation")
```

5.3.3. Suggestion of Rules

Shared resource dependencies may lead to inconsistencies during the collaboration when results are accessed simultaneously by two or more services. The coordination engine can help the human coordinator through detecting potential inconsistencies and suggesting rules to avoid them.

The output relation of a contribution to a result as defined in the composition model in Section 4.2 specifies which results, hence resources in the document, the associated service is allowed to update. The event model could contain an event for the association of a contribution with a result. Whenever an event of this type occurs, a rule might check whether another contribution already associates the result. The rule engine might warn the user and suggest a rule for task sequencing as shown in the previous section. The input relation of a contribution to a result defines which results an associated service might request as input. In order to avoid inconsistent reads and a service working on outdated input data, a rule might check on association of the contribution with the result whether the result is associated as output of another contribution. The action of the rule might warn the coordinator and propose a task sequencing rule.

The definition of powerful rules for the detection of additional rules for shared resource dependency management is subject of future work.

5.4. Conclusion and Discussion

The event model and coordination rule mechanism defined in the previous sections realize the design features specified in Chapter 3 as shown in Table 5.2.

Table 5.2.: Realization of design features through event model and coordination rule mechanism.

ID	Design Feature	Realization
DF 4-1	Provide extensible event model to support notification as base coordination mechanism.	New atomic events can be added to the event model presented in Section 5.2.
DF 4-2	Allow coordinators to specify rules based on events for different coordination mechanisms.	Coordination rule mechanism defines a language to specify ECA rules and a rule engine enabling rule-based participation protocol automation and collaboration-specific coordination mechanisms.

The event model presented in Section 5.2 in combination with the coordination rule mechanism allows collaboration systems to reduce required effort of human coordinators through semi-automation of protocols as well as the management of collaboration-specific dependencies in service compositions. While participation protocols support the coordination as regards the binding and execution of services in a composition, the coordination rule mechanism adds dependency management between participating services. A discussion on the participation protocol framework is provided in Section 5.1.3.

The *configuration of coordination* mechanisms to support different use cases can be performed by collaboration system providers or by coordinators of collaborations. Collaboration system providers can use the event model and actions as they are designed. Alternatively, they might create new event types and define action types which suit particular requirements of collaborations to be supported with the designed system. These event and action types are base for the rules which can be specified in the collaboration system. Collaboration system providers might also specify particular rules, e.g., for protocol automation, which are applied throughout the system. Finally, collaboration system providers specify the available participation protocols for a system. The specifications in the collaboration system frame the activities which can be performed by participants of a system. Coordinators might configure coordination through specifying rules.

ECA rules originally were applied in the context of active databases [106] but also have been used for exception handling in workflows or on application-level to express reactive and adaptive behaviors and enable developers to tailor applications to their domain needs [30]. Moreover, ECA rules are used in knowledge management since humans are familiar with thinking in ECA rules and at the same time ECA rules allow for formal representation in systems [12, p. 73]. In addition, the combination of event-driven with service-oriented architectures enables the implementation of agile and adaptive business processes based on service composition [19, p. 38]. In the collaboration model, the rule mechanism enables flexible configuration and specification of collaboration-specific behavior, e.g., a rule can be added or removed anytime during collaboration by a human coordinator. Services are loosely coupled via rules. This flexibility is useful to support evolving, hardly predictable service compositions as described in the composition model. The flexibility, however, might result in conflicts and inconsistencies. A large set of rules might diminish usability for the human coordinators. The rule language is powerful which complicates its use for human coordinators. Mechanisms for efficient rule management and conflict handling usable for collaboration participants are subject of future work.

Rules allow for *automation* of tasks in a collaboration. Automation can be defined as the automated execution of tasks which could be performed by humans [104]. On the one hand, automation supports coordination tasks of human coordinators, e.g., through rules which notify about dependencies and potential inconsistencies or automatically make service calls. On the other hand, automation increases coordination overhead, e.g., if software services are included to perform specific tasks. Collaboration system providers have to design protocols which can be understood and supported by all participants, humans and non-humans. Which tasks should be automated has to be decided for each use case, or even collaboration. Different aspects might influence this decision (cf. [105]). For example, the mental and physical workload of participants might be decreased through automation. On the other hand, participants might loose awareness of events happening during collaboration. Additional criteria are costs of automation, e.g., in case of wrong automation rules, or trust in automated systems by the end-user [105]. The rule mechanism aims to support semi-automation and dependency management rather than full automation of processes. In the collaboration model, the end-user can co-decide on the degree of automation. For example, participants can decide which steps in the protocols to automate. This might have a positive effect on trust as long as the rule base stays usable.

To examine whether the collaboration model is feasible and can be implemented using service composition technologies, an infrastructure and a collaboration application realize a version of the collaboration model as presented in the following chapter.

Part III.

Implementation and Evaluation

6. Proof of Concept: Design and Implementation

This chapter introduces the design and implementation of a collaboration system which demonstrates feasibility of the collaboration model. The collaboration model is mapped on a software architecture and implemented in a Web-based software prototype. The system contains the *collaboration infrastructure* realizing data source and application logic of the system and the *collaboration application* realizing a user front end which illustrates how to use the infrastructure to support humans during collaborative document creation. Besides the collaboration model features, the infrastructure supports the implementation of various adapters, e.g., for Web services which serve as input sources to collaborations. Figure 6.1 presents an overview of the software architecture.

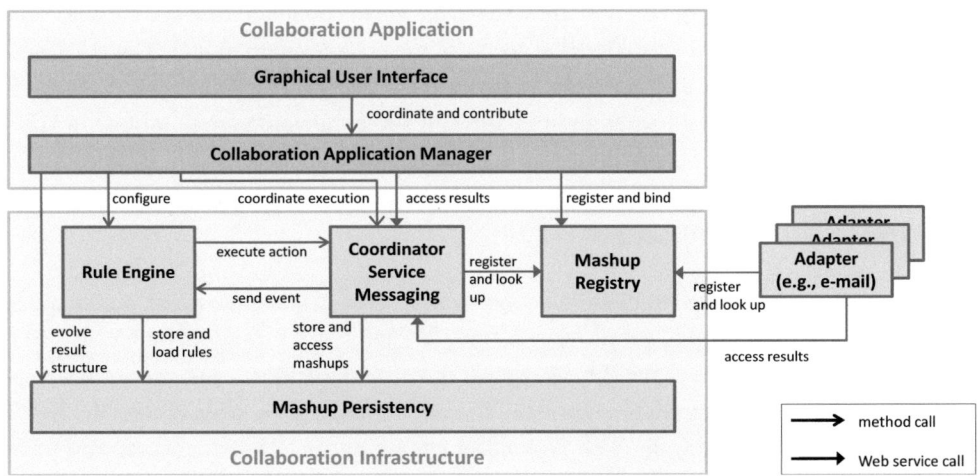

Figure 6.1.: Architecture overview of the collaboration system.

The collaboration application on the upper part of the figure provides a *GUI* for coordinators to create result structures as well as for human contributors to provide services. Software services can be provided through external *adapters* as shown on the right hand side. As part of the collaboration infrastructure, the *mashup persistency* stores result structures created by coordinators as well as rules associated with a collaboration. The term "mashup" in the name of the component stems from the fact that the documents are service compositions which are created by the end-users suiting their current need. The *coordinator service messaging* component provides a Web service interface to the results in the mashup persistency which is used by contributors (e.g., using service adapters or the collaboration application) to retrieve and update result contents. In addition, the coordinator service messaging component is responsible for executing participation protocols, e.g., calls services on request of a coordinator through the collaboration application. To perform this functionality, the coordinator service messaging component accesses the *mashup registry* to retrieve information about providers, services, and their endpoints. The mashup registry allows providers to register and offer services, e.g., through an adapter or the collaboration application. The coordinator service messaging component might send events to the *rule engine*, e.g., in case of state changes in a protocol or changes on the result tree. The rule engine, which is configured with rules by the coordinators, analyzes the rules and might execute actions using the the coordinator service messaging component. The infrastructure components are detailed in Section 6.1, followed by an overview of the application and select adapters in Section 6.2.

A guiding principle during design and development of the collaboration system was to use mature standards and existing technologies and components where possible. Another, in some cases contradictory, guiding principle was to design the collaboration system adaptable as regards the extension and specialization points of the collaboration model. The collaboration system thus represents a compromise between these two guiding principles.

Earlier versions of the collaboration infrastructure and application are described in [126] and [127].

6.1. Infrastructure Architecture

The infrastructure is designed as distributed hypermedia system using the REST architectural style [47]. REST uses simple, yet proven abstractions and has a low adoption barrier [108] and might therefore support scalability as regards involved participants and adapter developers. Web standards and technologies like HTTP, URI, or XML are used to realize the REST principles. On the one hand, the Web provides a large number of heterogeneous resources which could be utilized in collaboration. On the other hand, if documents realized during collaboration are offered through Web technologies they might be more easily spread and reused on the Web.

RESTful systems realize the principles (a) resource identification, (b) manipulation of resources through representations, (c) self-descriptive messages, and (d) HATEOAS [47, p. 82]. When using Web technologies, each *resource is identified* and addressed through a URI. Resources can be accessed and manipulated through a *uniform interface* with a fixed set of operations. In HTTP, these operations are PUT (create or update resource), GET (retrieve state of resource), POST (update state), and DELETE (remove). The operations are performed using *representations* of resources including data, e.g., the current state of the resource, and meta-data describing the data, e.g., its format. Each message is *self-descriptive*, i.e., contains all information required for the execution of a request, e.g., an update of a resource state. State of the application can be changed through following hyperlinks included in representations [47, p. 86ff.]

In the design of the collaboration infrastructure, contributions are represented as resources which can be accessed at their URI and manipulated through a uniform interface. Results produced during collaboration are represented as resources as well. A collaboration consists of a set of such resources which are composed by end-users in a flexible manner. Contributions are requested and performed through exchanging resource representations which change the state of contribution and result resources. Following the guiding principle to reuse mature standards, communication is performed using a subset of standard HTTP verbs. Messages are formatted in XML format.

Storage and manipulation of resources as well as maintenance of application state is supported by four infrastructure components. The components realize collaboration model features as follows.

- The *mashup registry* enables providers to publish profiles and service types according to the component model described in Section 4.1. Coordinators can search and find suitable providers and services. The registry supports human and software-based services alike. In addition, the registry is responsible for storing state of service binding protocols.

- The *mashup persistency* stores resources of result documents produced during service composition and serves as a central access point for all participants to the collaboration results.

- The *coordinator service messaging* component supports correct execution of service execution protocols, e.g., accessing document parts as well as implements communication with providers. The component implements the set of basic protocols defined in Section 5.1.

- The *rule engine* component allows coordinators to specify rules as well as executes them on occurrence of events following the coordination rule mechanism specified in Section 5.3.

In addition to the four infrastructure components, the collaboration system offers an *adapter framework* which enables developers to implement service adapters according to the component model. The infrastructure components and the adapter framework are described in Sections 6.1.2 to 6.1.6.

6.1.1. Service Interfaces

Service providers are responsible for delivering services on demand. The infrastructure prescribes the interface service providers and services have to offer in order to contribute in a
collaboration. The design of the interface involved the following considerations.

- The interface should represent providers offering several resources through a service
  interface according to the component model described in Section 4.1.

- The interface should provide access to provided resources, i.e., implement the request()
  method of the service class in the component model. If the resource is not yet available,
  the same method should request its creation to avoid that requesters need to distinguish
  between requesting a creation or an update of a resource.

- Providers should be able to update the resource if it is requested, e.g., adapt it to the
  collaboration it is requested for, and return it asynchronously. Asynchronous response
  is especially useful for human providers.

- Since results also are represented as resources, the URI scheme should represent the
  result structure for navigation in the result tree.

The infrastructure design differentiates between *service instances* and *providers*. Service
instances are resources which can be accessed at a unique URI using a uniform API and
represent a contribution in a collaboration. Providers are responsible for offering this API.
Providers might be humans or software systems.

Service instances can be accessed using their URI. Each URI follows the scheme {pro-
vider URI}/{mashup ID}/.../{contribution ID}. The scheme represents the result
tree structure of the mashup the contribution is associated with. The entry point for each
query is {server URI}/{mashup ID}/ where mashup ID is replaced with the unique identifier of the mashup. The results on the first level of the result structure are appended according to the scheme {server URI}/{mashup ID}/{result ID}/ where result ID is
replaced with the unique identifier of the result. Accordingly, for subresults, the scheme
{server URI}/{mashup ID}/{result ID}/ {result ID} is used. Three dots (/.../)
in URIs represent an arbitrary number of result IDs in the path representing a deep result
structure.

Table 6.1 shows the provider API available for service instances which contains one single
operation. The operation is used by coordinators to request or create a service instance.
In order to implement the request() method of the service class in the component model, a
service instance can be requested using PUT on its URI. In HTTP, traditionally the GET
operation is used to "retrieve a representation of a resource" [116, p. 97]. For the request of a

service instance, however, the PUT method is chosen because a request changes the state of a resource according to the service execution protocols. For example, a request might change the state of a service instance from bound to requested. A service instance thus represents the execution of one contribution in one collaboration. The PUT operation contains information about the contribution to be delivered, e.g., service type or input results. If a service instance at the given URI does not exist, the PUT operation causes the creation of the service instance through the provider.

Table 6.1.: Provider API.

Operation	URI or Template	Description
PUT	`{provider URI}/{mashup ID}/.../{con-tribution ID}`	Request a result as contribution. Asynchronously responds to requester. Creates resource if it does not exist.

Having received a request, a service instance performs the contribution which might involve calls to external Web services or software systems or human activities. The result of these activities are sent back to the coordinator in an asynchronous manner. A detailed discussion of the interactions between coordinators and service instances and the exchanged information is provided in Section 6.1.4.

Existing services which should be used to contribute in collaborations need to be encapsulated into adapters. In addition, adapters for human-provided service instances might be required which enable humans to use their favorite tool for service provisioning. Adapters might add support for storing a copy of the mashup or automatically managing participation protocols. Section 6.1.6 discusses those additional features and presents a framework for developers to construct adapters.

Coordinators of a collaboration need to find providers and service instances for participation in their collaboration. Similarly, service providers might want to find data on collaborations they could participate in. Therefore, information about available mashups and providers is stored in a mashup registry as described in the following section.

6.1.2. Mashup Registry

SOAs commonly provide a service registry in order to allow service providers to publish and advertise their services. Potential clients can discover those services [7, p. 151]. An example is Universal Description Discovery & Integration (UDDI), a standardization effort for a registry for services primarily described using WS-* standards [93]. Services regis-

tered in UDDI are categorized, e.g., according to the business they support or to user defined taxonomies. This categorization allows clients to browse lists of services similar to
yellow pages. In addition, UDDI stores detailed technical information on how to invoke a
service [7, p. 175]. A registry for services and APIs provided with arbitrary technologies is
ProgrammableWeb[13].

Allowing coordinators of a collaboration to find potential participants and learn how to
invoke them is a desired feature in the collaboration system. Accordingly, the infrastructure
contains the mashup registry. The design of the mashup registry involved the following
considerations.

- Existing registries mainly focus on software services. The mashup registry should
  allow to store information on services provided by humans as well as software services.

- The registry should contain informal information about providers allowing coordinators to search for capabilities. Additionally, the registry should store structured data
  required to address and invoke a service instance.

- The mashup registry should enable publication of information on open contributions
  or collaborations where anyone can participate. This information could be used by
  human providers to volunteer to participate in specific collaborations.

- Services instances which are registered in a registry have a state, e.g., they are requested for a particular collaboration. These states represent the state of participation
  protocols. Information about service states is therefore also relevant to coordinators
  and thus should be stored in the registry for lookup.

- The mashup registry should be realized using REST principles, more precisely Web
  technologies. This approach promises easier access to, manipulation of, and navigation through registry entries. In addition, the Web browser already provides a basic
  interface for humans to navigate through and search in the registry.

According to these design considerations, the mashup registry presented in this section is
responsible for (a) enabling service and mashup discovery and addressing as well as (b) me-
diating service binding protocols through storing state information of services. The mashup
registry consists of a database as well as accessors providing a REST API to the records
stored in the database. Figure 6.2 presents the domain model of the mashup registry which
is mapped on the database structure. The stored elements support the two responsibilities of
the registry as described in the following.

---

[13]http://www.programmableweb.com/ (accessed January 2nd, 2013)

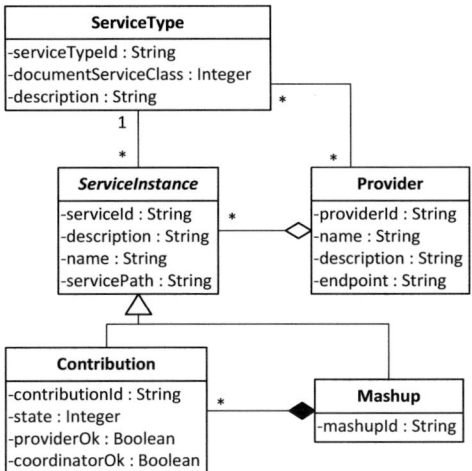

Figure 6.2.: Domain model of the mashup registry.

- Service discovery is supported based on the storage of descriptions of provider profiles and service types. The registry offers interfaces for service providers to store and publish descriptions of service types they offer. In addition, the registry enables coordinators to search and find service providers.

  Providers are stored along with a description of their profile as well as an endpoint to address them during service execution. The endpoint can be changed anytime during collaboration which decouples the provider and the mashup and makes it easier to relocate a provider.

  Service types provide a description as well as a document service class which represents the characteristics of a service with respect to a collaboration. The service type follows an open taxonomy of service types. Example service types are content provisioning and transformation. Providers might associate with service types they provide.

  Components for participant discovery in human collaboration include expert systems or mechanisms like selection based on shortest to-do list. Often, participants are found in face-to-face communication. A sophisticated approach for service discovery is not a main focus of this thesis. Therefore, coordinators are supported by a simple capability-based discovery and selection approach based on the categorization of offered services according to their service type.

  In addition to the generic providers and service types, the registry stores elements associated with a collaboration as *service instances*. Two types of service instances exist, mashups and contributions. *Mashups* are stored in order to allow potential providers to search for and find collaborations they wish to participate in. An interested provider could navigate to open contributions in a mashup and apply for them through setting the state according to the binding protocol. *Contributions* represent concrete services delivered in a collaboration.

The abstract class service instance defines attributes for mashups and service instances stored in the registry. Each service instance has a name, a description, and a servicePath. In combination with the endpoint of the provider, the servicePath represents the full address to the service instance which can be used to call the service instance. If the endpoint of the service provider changes, the provider does not have to update the address information of all provided service instances.

- The registry additionally acts as a *mediator* for the interaction between coordinator and provider during the execution of the service binding protocols. For example, coordinators and providers interact when a coordinator asks a provider to accept a contribution. For each contribution, an entry is stored in the registry along with a state attribute which represents the current state of the contribution. Whoever initiates the interaction in a protocol, associates a contribution with a provider. Parties indicate their agreement for the binding as a flag of the contribution. The flag coordinatorOk (providerOk) is used in order to denote that the coordinator (provider) agrees with the binding or not.

Which states a contribution can have depends on the protocol logic followed by the participants. The registry, however, is not able to ensure that the contribution state is correctly set. The control of the protocol is left to protocol engines which might extend the registry. The infrastructure as described in this thesis implements the coordinator-initiated binding protocol as well as the self-service binding protocol as described in Section 5.1.1.

Since all states of all contributions are stored in the registry, providers do not have to store contribution states. As a result, providers are decoupled and independent of protocol changes which might occur during collaboration. In addition, storing contribution states in a registry separate from the collaboration contents allows participants to retrieve personal to-do lists across collaboration systems with different persistencies. Coordinators can inspect contribution state and decide on further actions, e.g., requesting the contribution. In addition, coordinators might publish open contributions across collaboration system boundaries.

Changes to the state of a contribution are not pushed to providers or coordinators. Therefore, the registry provides an interface to query all binding requests, e.g., by a provider.

The registry can be accessed via a REST API. The interface provides access to the representations of various resources and provides standard REST operations in order to manipulate the resources. The resource classes are mashup, contribution, provider, and service type. For each resource class, a container resource exists enabling access to the complete set of resources of the class. Each resource (container resources and all individual resources) can be addressed and accessed via a dedicated URI. The URIs of the container resources are supposed to be globally known. All other URIs of individual resources are communicated within resource representations and must not be constructed by clients as the underlying URI schema might change at any time. The messages exchanged during communication, e.g., for setting a contribution state, with the registry are representations of the resources in well-defined content types. The representations are hypermedia documents in XML format including links for navigation, e.g., from a list of mashups to a single mashup. The API operations of container resources and resources are listed in Table 6.2.

Table 6.2.: Registry API for container and individual resources.

Operation	URI or Template	Description
GET	/{container resource name}	Retrieve a (possibly empty) list of resources. Results can be restricted by specifying query parameters. A specific resource can be searched for by specifying its ID as a query parameter. The list includes a short description and the resource URI of each resource. The return status is always OK if the URI is correct.
POST	/{container resource name}	Create a new individual resource. Requires the representation of a resource as input and returns the representation of the created resource. The return status is OK if the resource could be created. The status might be FORBIDDEN, e.g., if a resource already exists or representations are not consistent.
GET	/{container resource name}/{resource ID}	Retrieve a representation of the resource with all details. Might lead to UNKNOWN status.

Continued on next page

Table 6.2 – *Continued from previous page*

Operation	URI or template	Description
PUT	/{container resource name}/{resource ID}	Update the individual resource. Requires the representation of a resource as input and returns the representation of the updated resource. Might lead to UNKNOWN status. Might lead to FORBIDDEN status, e.g., if the representation message is not consistent.
DELETE	/{container resource name}/{resource ID}	Delete the resource. Might lead to UNKNOWN status.

Choosing the REST architectural style for the realization of the registry brings advantages like easy navigation for participants in order to find information, e.g., between providers and service types. In addition, the GET function for containers implements a search functionality which can be tailored by providing search parameters. The implementation of clients with user interfaces should be easy since the interface is limited to a small number of functions. Human providers can then easily add their information in natural language. Since the registry is implemented as a hypermedia system, it potentially can be distributed as long as the entry point URI is known to clients.

The registry is implemented as a J2EE application running on an Apache Tomcat Web application container[14]. All data records are stored in MySQL[15] database using the Hibernate[16] persistency framework.

The registry enables service and mashup discovery and managing binding protocols. Mashups themselves are stored in the mashup persistency as described in the following.

6.1.3. Mashup Persistency

The mashup persistency represents the data layer of the infrastructure architecture and is responsible for storing all elements belonging to a collaboration. The design of the mashup persistency involved the following considerations.

- The mashup persistency should store (a) collaboration structures, i.e., results with associated contributions and coordinators according to the composition model presented

---

[14]http://tomcat.apache.org/ (accessed January 2nd, 2013)
[15]http://www.mysql.de/ (accessed January 2nd, 2013)
[16]http://www.hibernate.org/ (accessed January 2nd, 2013)

in Section 4.2, and (b) unstructured content of created documents, e.g., text, model fragments, or multimedia. As regards storing the structure of collaborations, the persistency is realized based on a traditional relational database design. A reason for this decision is that the database has to store data with sophisticated dependencies which is not expected to change frequently in its structure, e.g., the result hierarchy and association to other model elements like contributions. Additional arguments are the high maturity of publicly available relational database systems. In addition, frameworks and tools for object-relational mapping, code generation, and version control of stored data could be used for implementation. Relational databases are able to store large texts as potentially required in document content. Additional file formats, e.g., pictures or videos, can be stored on Web servers and referenced from within the result structure.

- Together with the result structure, the mashup persistency should store rules belonging to a mashup. Data of one mashup can be managed and accessed at a central location, e.g., by the collaboration applications which represents all information on a mashup in one GUI. In addition, the rule engine described in Section 6.1.5, for which an existing component was used, does not store rules in case of shutdown. As the rule engine does not come with a database, the database in the persistency can be used.

The described functionality of the mashup persistency is used by a number of infrastructure components as shown in Figure 6.1. The mashup persistency offers an interface to the collaboration application to create and modify result structures as well as associate contributions. The rule engine stores and loads rules from the persistency. In addition, the coordinator service messaging accesses the persistency to retrieve and write results through a service interface.

Figure 6.3 shows the domain model of the persistency which is based on the conceptual collaboration model presented in Section 4.2. Instances of the domain model elements are stored in tables. The elements are described in the following.

- A *document service* in general represents an atomic activity which can be executed and provides a resource as outcome. The resource can be any document fragment. Since all information on a document service is stored in the mashup registry as service instance, the persistency only contains a link to the entry in the registry in the service ID field. Document services might be called by actions in a rule or emit events. A document service either is a contribution or a result.

- A *contribution* represents the participation in a collaboration by means of performing an atomic activity. As soon as a contribution entry is created in the persistency, an entry for this contribution is published in the registry and associated through the service ID

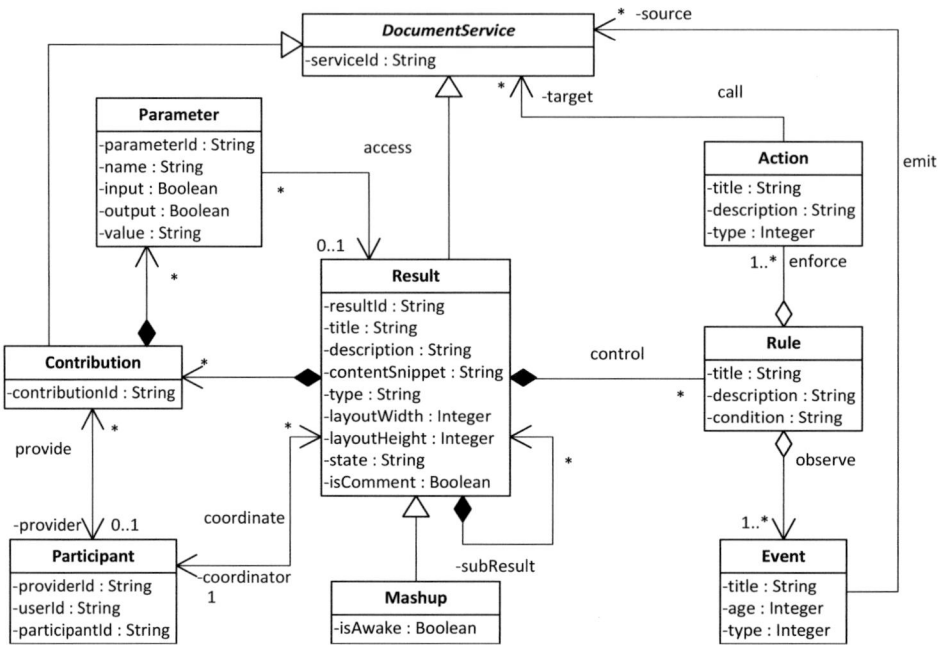

Figure 6.3.: Domain model of the mashup persistency.

with the persistency entry. Details on a contribution, e.g., a task description, thus are stored only in the registry.

A contribution is associated with a set of *parameters* which link them to input results required to carry out the task. Some parameters associate results which might be changed during service execution. In addition, parameters might specify a value required to perform the activity, e.g., a search string for a search service.

- A *participant* might act as a provider of a contribution and/or as a coordinator for a result. Participants might be associated with a provider stored in the registry as well as a user in a collaboration application.

- A *result* represents the outcome of an activity that is carried out by one or more participants of the collaboration, the providers. A result is associated with exactly one coordinator who is responsible for associating contributions and providers. A coordinator might also delegate coordinator responsibilities to other participants.

Besides a title and description, a result might specify layout information like height and width in order to position the result in a user interface. The result might be in a state according to the participation protocols. If the content of a result is a comment, the result might be skipped for publication.

A result is a leaf of a document and stores document contents produced and changed throughout the collaboration by contributions in a contentSnippet. The type of contents might indicate characteristics that could be useful for processing, e.g., rendering. A result is a document service, i.e., the content of each result is accessible by means of REST service calls as explained in the following section.

A *mashup* is the root of a document. A mashup can be asleep meaning that processing of rules for the mashup is shut down in order to allow for sensitive design activities. The awake state of a mashup can be changed by coordinators through the collaboration application.

- A *rule* is stored along with a meaningful title and description as well as a condition. On startup of the rule processor, the rule engine retrieves all rules for a mashup and loads them into the memory of the rule processor. A rule is associated with at least one action and one event. An action can be of type request or accept binding. An event might have a document service as source. In addition, it has an age and a type according to the event model presented in Section 5.2. The infrastructure implementation realizes various event types representing states in binding and execution protocols.

The mashup persistency was implemented through the generation of an Eclipse Modeling Framework (EMF)[17] model from the UML domain model. The EMF model served as input to the persistency framework Hibernate which generates tables as well as accessor classes in Java to create, update, delete, and version content in the tables. Data is stored in a MySQL database. As regards formats of contents, the infrastructure supports storage of text with a maximum of 4 billion characters. Multimedia content can be included through storing hyperlinks in the contentSnippet. Queries on the contents are not supported in the current implementation.

Version control of result data of is realized in an earlier version of the mashup persistency in order to enable traceability and reversability of changes. At each change, the persistency stores an entry of the current state of the object as well as the changes required to return to the previous entry as delta. While versions are stored, mechanisms on top, e.g., roll-back of changes, are left to future work.

The persistency is a representation of collaboration state as regards result structure, associated contributions, and participants. The provisioning of results through providers is supported by the coordinator service messaging component described in the following section.

---

[17]http://www.eclipse.org/modeling/emf/ (accessed January 2nd, 2013)

6.1.4. Coordinator Service Messaging

The coordinator service messaging is responsible for ensuring correct and consistent state transitions regarding execution of participation protocols. This includes (a) supporting input retrieval by providers, (b) sending requests to service instances, and (c) managing responses of requested service instances. The design of the coordinator service messaging component involved the following considerations.

- Results might contain subresults. Complete result structures might be reused in other collaborations. The component therefore should provide a mechanism to access a subtree of a result structure as service.

- Result content might be sensitive. Therefore, authorization mechanisms are required for read and write requests on results.

- In order to be able to reuse results in other collaborations, they should be offered as services with the same interface as services offered by external providers.

Figure 6.4 presents an overview of the coordinator service messaging component as well as its interrelations with other infrastructure components and services. The parts of the service messaging component are described in the following.

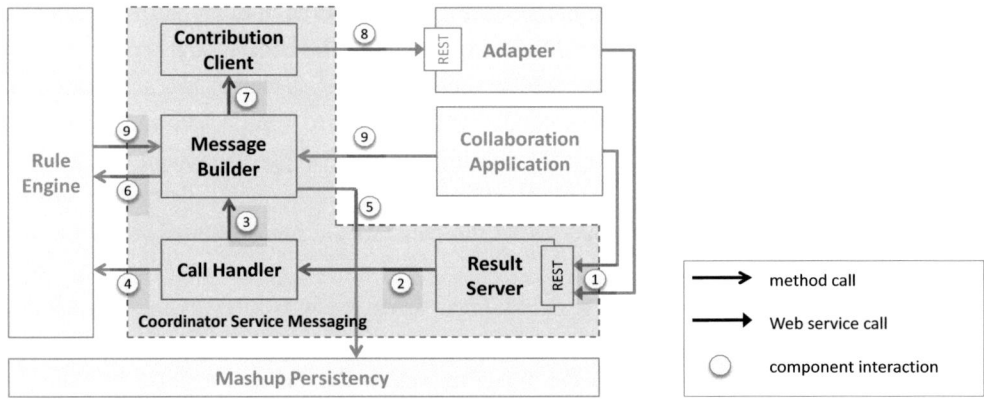

Figure 6.4.: Overview of the coordinator service messaging component.

As part of the coordinator service messaging component, the *result server* provides a REST API for accessing result content stored in the mashup persistency during processing of *input retrieval protocols* and *service responses*. Accordingly, result contents can be retrieved and manipulated through a service interface. The API enables contributors to read and write result contents during a collaboration. The result structure and attributes can not be changed via the API but using the mashup persistency. Users of the API are service providers contributing to the collaboration as well as the collaboration application.

The result server dynamically creates URIs for results. The URIs follow the URI scheme presented in Section 6.1.1. Each GET request on a result URI returns a hypermedia document including the actual content of the result as well as a list of URIs of all child results which enables the traversal through the result tree structure. A PUT request updates the contents of the result. A DELETE request removes result content.

Figure 6.4 illustrates the flow of interactions between the components during requests on results content. Interaction 1 denotes the receipt of a request, e.g., a GET on a specific result. As soon as receiving a request, the result server directs the request to the *call handler* (interaction 2). The call handler is responsible for checking whether the requester is authorized. Authorization can be implemented in at least two ways.

- First, the call handler emits events for result service requests to the rule engine which checks for authorization based on ECA rules (interaction 4). The rule engine might check whether the requester is associated with a contribution which points to the requested result. In addition, role-based access control or constraints like separation of duties (two results might be written only by two different providers) or temporal restriction of accessing a result might be implemented using rules [23]. The rule engine might access an external authentication component to check proof access and authentication rights.

- In the second realization variant, authorization is based on the association of the requester as provider to a contribution which has the requested result either as input or output. The call handler checks this constraint and allows the request or rejects it.

While the first variant is more powerful, coordinators are required to specify authorization rules for all results, contributions, or participants they define in their collaboration. In addition, the rule base grows with each created element in the mashup persistency and needs to be managed by coordinators in order to stay up to date and consistent. This might result in a coordination overhead and reduce usability. The rule engine needs to be extended with additional event and action types. Therefore, and since authorization is not a main focus of this thesis, the latter variant is realized in the infrastructure.

After authorization, the call handler requests the *message builder* (interaction 3) which is responsible for constructing the response message for the requester. If the authorization is positive, the message builder accesses the mashup persistency and performs the requested activity, i.e., retrieve, create, update, or delete result content (interaction 5). The message builder might emit events, e.g., on update of a result (interaction 6), to the rule engine.

Finally, the response message is handed over to the *contribution client* (interaction 7) which sends it to the requester (interaction 8), i.e., a provider or a collaboration application.

Interactions 1 to 8 describe how input retrieval protocols can be handled by the infrastructure. In the following, more details on *service execution* are presented. Service instance calls might be triggered either by a human coordinator through the collaboration application or by a rule in the rule engine (interaction 9). Figure 6.5 shows an overview of the activities performed by the coordinator service messaging component and an adapter during execution of a service request/response protocol. The adapter is a provider which executes custom code to perform an activity, e.g., calls a Web service.

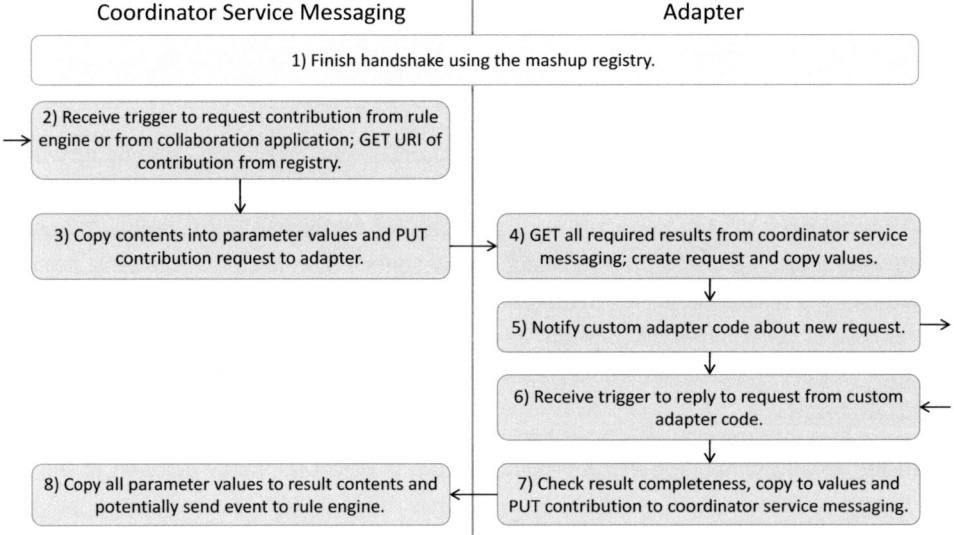

Figure 6.5.: Sequence of interactions between the coordinator service messaging component and a provider adapter for service execution.

A human coordinator or a rule trigger the call of a contribution. Subsequently, the contribution client retrieves the servicePath of the contribution and the endpoint of the provider from the registry and sends a PUT request to the composed URI according to the API defined in Section 6.1.1. As shown in Listing 6.1 the message sent with the PUT request includes references to the results which might be received as input as well as the results which are allowed to be written by the adapter.

The adapter can now retrieve result contents as described previously from the coordinator service messaging component (interaction 1 in Figure 6.4). The adapter might call external Web services. When the adapter finished producing results associated with the contribution, it pushes the content via PUT to the output results specified in the request message (interaction 1 in Figure 6.4). The coordinator service messaging processes the PUT request as described previously, starting with interaction 2 and might then set the state of the contribution in the registry according to the protocol used during collaboration, e.g., "responded".

```
<ContributionRequest>
 <Service title="write description" contributionId="writeDescription">
  <Description>pls write project description</Description>
 </Service>
 <Parameter name="input" in="true" out="false">
  <value>http://kit.edu/mashup-manager/projectProposal</value>
 </Parameter>
 <Parameter name="output" in="false" out="true">
  <value>http://kit.edu/mashup-manager/projectProposal/
      projectDescription </value>
 </Parameter>
</ContributionRequest>
```

Listing 6.1: Example message for service request.

To summarize, the service execution, i.e., request and response of a service instance, are decoupled and can be performed asynchronously, for instance, if a human provider has to write a paragraph of a document. In addition, the decoupling allows providers to PUT several results for one contribution at different times. A PUT on the results can be repeated, e.g., if a provider produced an updated version of the content.

The previously described behavior of the coordinator service messaging is about result retrieval as well as service request and response. In order to allow for *reuse* of results, the infrastructure needs to support the interface described in Section 6.1.1 for results. The PUT method of each result therefore is overloaded. Based on the message sent with the PUT request, the call handler decides on the response. In case of a contribution request message like the one presented in Listing 6.1, the call handler triggers an asynchronous response to the specified results. In case the message specifies an update of a result resource as response to a request, the call handler triggers an update of the result.

To summarize, the collaboration service messaging component provides the interface as shown in Table 6.3. The interface allows the execution of services as well as the reuse of produced results.

Table 6.3.: API of the coordinator service messaging component.

Operation	URI or Template	Description
GET	/{mashup URI} /.../{result ID}	Retrieve resources of a result, i.e., result content. Returns a representation of mashup, result, or NOT FOUND in case resource does not exist.

Continued on next page

Table 6.3 – *Continued from previous page*

Operation	URI or template	Description
PUT	/{mashup URI} /.../{result ID}	Update content of the result at the given path. The message contains a result representation including contents. Might lead to UNKNOWN status.
DELETE	/{mashup URI} /.../{result ID}	Delete content of a result at the given path. Might lead to UNKNOWN status.
PUT	/{mashup URI} /.../{result ID}	Request a result as contribution. Asynchronously responds to requester. Returns NOT FOUND in case resource does not exist.

The realization of the service execution protocols is complex, since the protocols have to represent the asynchronous working style of humans. Pushing outcomes to a mashup requires access and rights management mechanisms in order to ensure that only results are written which the provider is allowed to write. Authorization is realized in a limited version based on input and output parameters. Future developments of the infrastructure might include advanced authorization and access right mechanisms.

The coordinator service messaging component enables contributors to access results in a collaboration. Contributors, however, are only allowed to create, update, or delete result contents. A result can only be deleted from a mashup by coordinators which might decrease usability of the approach. In a future design of the component, creation or deletion of results might be feature of the REST API.

The component supports the example protocols for input retrieval as well as service request-response protocol described in Section 5.1.2. In order to realize additional service execution protocols, e.g., with approvals, the call handler has to be extended with additional logic.

The coordinator service messaging component is realized as Java application and deployed in an Apache Tomcat servlet container. The coordinator service messaging component supports interaction protocols for coordinating communication between coordinators and providers. In the following, the rule engine is described which supports the specification of additional coordination requirements.

6.1.5. Rule Engine

The rule engine is responsible for driving automatic enforcement of rules specified during collaboration. The rule engine monitors messages, checks the occurrence of particular event patterns, and triggers the sending of messages as a consequence. The design of the rule engine involved the following considerations.

- An existing engine for executing rules should be used, since the development of a sophisticated rule engine is not focus of this thesis. Different collaboration use cases require different rules, event types, and actions to be performed. The engine should therefore provide an interface to create rules as well as specify event types and actions.

- The rule engine should offer an API to submit events, e.g., to be accessed by the coordination service messaging component.

- Coordinators of a collaboration should be enabled to start or stop the processing of rules for a specific collaboration.

Figure 6.6 shows an overview of the internal components of the rule engine as realized in the collaboration infrastructure. For the realization of the rule engine, the complex event processing (CEP) engine ESPER[18] was chosen because it allows developers to specify own event

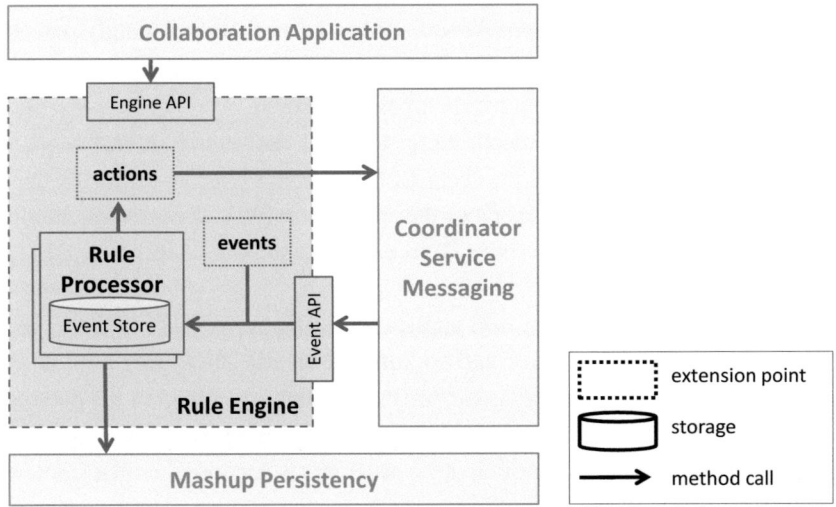

Figure 6.6.: Overview of the rule engine.

types as classes including event attributes as well as actions performing collaboration-specific functionality. ESPER promises to provide real-time event pattern detection and action execution. In addition, ESPER provides a rule specification language – the Event Processing

---

[18]http://esper.codehaus.org/(accessed January 2nd, 2013)

Language (EPL). Originally designed for sophisticated high-frequency event streams, EPL is a rich language addressing different demands of coordination rules like logical and temporal event correlation.

The rule engine provides two interfaces, the engine API and the event API.

- The engine API allows collaboration applications to start and stop rule processing for specific mashups as well as add and modify rules. Rules are mapped to EPL. Future versions of the rule engine might check the rule for compliance or consistency before storing them in the mashup persistency.

- Through the *event API*, event messages can be sent to the engine, e.g., by the coordinator service messaging component.

Rules as well as events are correlated to *rule processors*, i.e., for each collaboration exactly one rule processor exists. Separated rule processors allow coordinators to start and stop processing of rules for one collaboration without affecting other collaborations in a collaboration system. The rule processor is able to process complex events. If a rule processor is stopped, events for the collaboration might be stored in an event store. The infrastructure defines a set of event types, e.g., ServiceResponded and ContributionBound, as well as an action type able to send service calls to service instances. The infrastructure, however, can be extended with additional events and action types as required.

The rule engine supports simple processing of rules like sequencing or reminders. Future versions of the rule engine might offer the event API as a service interface allowing the engine to listen for additional events from outside of the application [30]. These events might allow collaborations to react on triggers coming from external systems or services, e.g., project management tools.

The rule engine is implemented as Java application using the ESPER API and deployed – together with the mashup persistency and coordinator service messaging – on an Apache Tomcat servlet container. The four infrastructure components described in the previous sections are implemented in a running prototype and support the coordination of collaboration. The implementation of adapters for participating providers is supported with a framework as described in the following.

6.1.6. Adapter Framework

The adapter framework is a Java programming framework that allows developers to write custom adapters, connecting different kinds of data sources or interactive applications to mashups. Adapters built with the adapter framework can be hosted on servlet containers like Apache Tomcat. Figure 6.7 presents an overview of the adapter framework architecture. The *adapter API* allows for programmatic access to the contribution store, the registry services, and the messaging services as explained in the following.

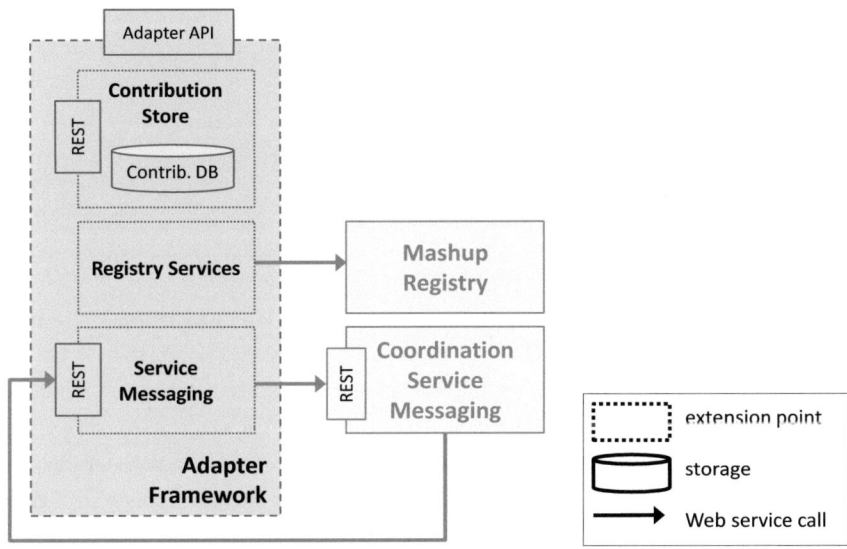

Figure 6.7.: Overview of the adapter framework.

In the *contribution store*, an adapter might store a copy of (parts of) mashups the provider participates in. Result content can then be evolved by providers in the contribution store and transferred back to the collaboration at a later point in time. In addition, content can be accessed when the collaboration server is not reachable.

The adapter framework offers a REST API to the stored mashup copies which is presented in Table 6.4.

Table 6.4.: Service instances API.

Operation	URI or Template	Description
GET	{provider URI}/{mashup ID}/.../{result ID}	Retrieve resources of a result, i.e., result content. Returns a representation of mashup, result, or NOT FOUND in case resource does not exist.

Continued on next page

Table 6.4 – *Continued from previous page*

Operation	URI or template	Description
PUT	{provider URI}/{mashup ID}/.../{result ID}	Update content of the result at the given path. The message contains a result representation including contents. Might lead to UNKNOWN status.
DELETE	{provider URI}/{mashup ID}/.../{result ID}	Delete content of a result at the given path. Might lead to UNKNOWN status.

Developers can build GUIs like text editors for different adapters using the API. Each result can be retrieved, updated, or deleted at the URI which represents the path to the result in the mashup structure. In addition, the collaboration infrastructure might push result content to adapters, e.g., in case of content updates.

The *registry services* provide access to the mashup registry in order to register the provider, service types, and service instances as well as query state of service instances. Service instances might be asked for binding by a coordinator which is denoted by the state asked-ForBinding in the service instance registry entry. Adapters might respond to this request automatically, e.g., through setting the state to bound. This feature is especially useful for automated software services. The adapter framework allows developers to enable automated binding through a configuration parameter.

The adapter framework provides basic functionality for communication with the infrastructure which can be extended in future work. Service instances have a state according to the collaboration they are used in. They are accessible at a specific URI which represents their location in the mashup structure. Service instances therefore can not easily be reused. Future versions of the adapter framework might provide support for copying or moving resources in order to reuse it in several collaborations. In addition, the adapter framework supports management of contributions of one provider. Editors, however, might require to be utilized by several users or tenants. Multi-tenancy should therefore be supported by future versions of the adapter framework. The creation of adapters with the adapter framework can only be done by software developers. Future work could address an adapter framework which can be configured by end-users.

Examples for service adapters are clients for humans (e.g., e-mail, Web client, rich client, mobile applications) or adapters to Web services or enterprise systems. Example service adapters for humans and software systems are presented in Section 6.2.3.

How the infrastructure components can be used to create a collaboration application including a GUI for human coordinators and contributors is illustrated in the following sections.

6.2. Collaboration Application and Graphical User Interface

Humans are the primary participants of a collaboration. They require an easy to use graphical interface enabling coordinators to outline document structures as well as contributors to provide results. The collaboration application leverages the infrastructure to realize an interface for human coordinators and contributors. While the collaboration application allows humans to use the infrastructure, adapters provide access to Web services which can perform valuable contributions to a collaboration. In the following sections, first an overview of the collaboration application is given followed by a discussion of three select service adapters.

6.2.1. Collaboration Application

Figure 6.8 presents an overview of the collaboration application architecture as described in the following.

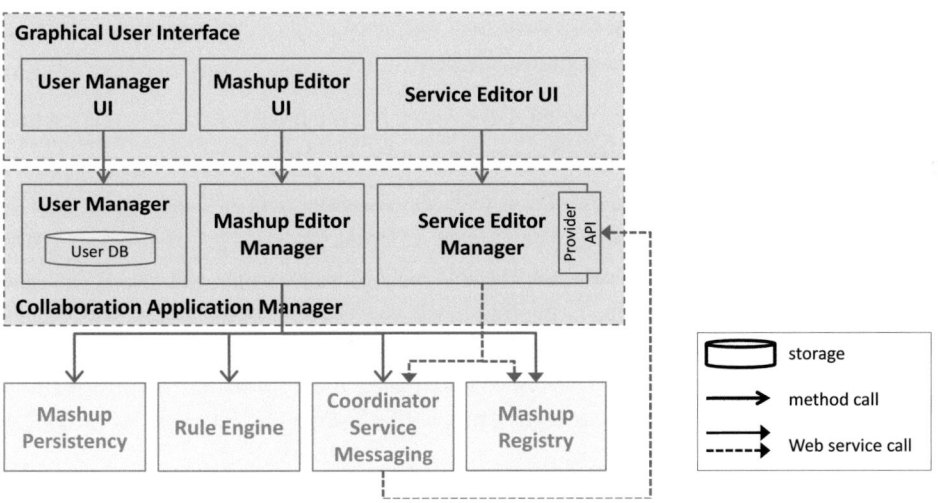

Figure 6.8.: Overview of the collaboration application.

The collaboration application manager offers a *user manager* to store users of the systems as well as support login functionality. Once a coordinator is logged in, the *mashup editor manager* enables him to (a) create a result hierarchy and assign contributions in the mashup persistency, (b) create rules and start/stop the rule engine for a collaboration in the rule engine, (c) perform steps in execution protocols like requesting services through the coordinator service messaging component as well as (d) store contributions and update contribution state according to participation protocols in the mashup registry.

While the mashup editor is used by coordinators, the *service editor manager* supports contributors of a collaboration. Once logged in, contributors can (e) request contributions they are assigned to as well as open contributions in the registry and update their state according to binding protocols, and (f) react to service requests. In order to receive service requests, e.g., by the coordinator service messaging component, the service editor manager offers a provider interface as described in Section 6.1.1.

6.2.2. Graphical User Interface

Coordinators and human providers access the collaboration application through their Web browser. The Web GUI integrates various components supporting document coordination, service provisioning, and user management use cases. The project proposal use case is used in the following to clarify the use cases supported by the application.

In order to support the collaboration, the application offers three GUIs.

- Fundamentally, the *user management user interface (UI)* allows all participants to log into the environment or register as a new user.

- Using the *mashup editor UI*, coordinators carry out the main document creation tasks. Figure 6.9 shows a screenshot of the experimental *mashup editor GUI*.

  The coordinator of the collaboration uses the *document coordination* tab. The editor represents and visualizes mashups from different perspectives of structure, participants, and document content. On the left hand side, mashups can be created, each representing a collaboration. In the figure, the coordinator selects the project proposal mashup. In the *element lists* panel, the coordinator defines the tree structure of the proposal document. In the *element details* panel, the coordinator identifies and assigns a provider who is able to write a motivation for the project proposal providing a description of the task.

  An overview of all participants and their contributions is presented in the *participating providers* panel. In the *coordination rules* panel the coordinator is enabled to specify rules using a graphical dialog interface for frequent rules, e.g., sequencing where a proofread service is called whenever the motivation is delivered. The rule engine for the mashup can be started by pushing the arrow button below the mashup list on the left side.

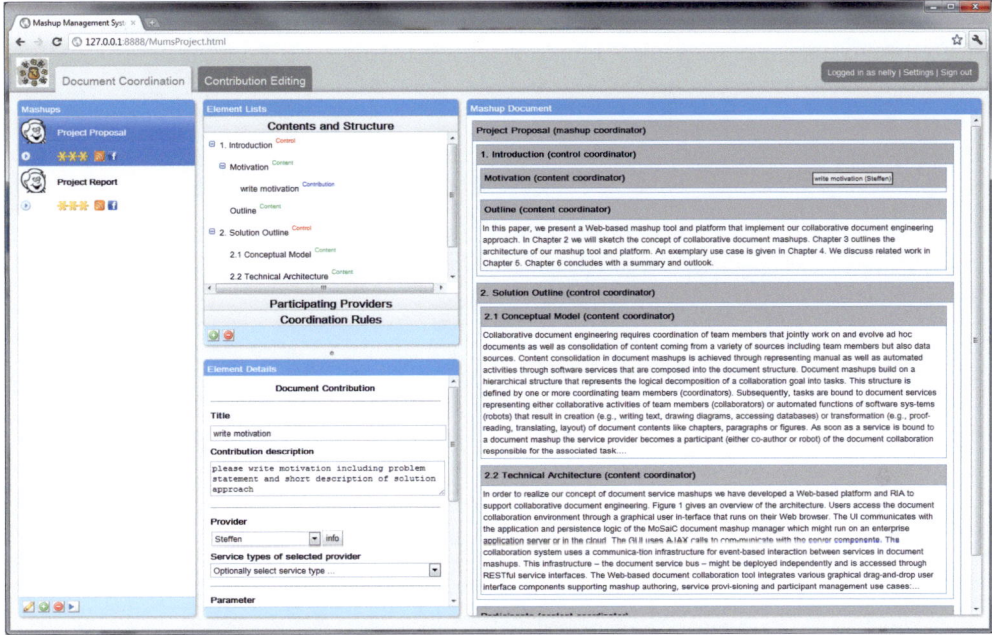

Figure 6.9.: Screenshot of the mashup editor UI.

The overall document structure including available contents is presented in the *mashup document* panel on the right side.

- In order to support contributors in providing services, the environment offers a *service editor UI*. Figure 6.10 shows a screenshot of the editor where the contributor received a request for writing the motivation for the project proposal.

  In the *contributions* panel on the left hand side, the service editor UI presents a personal to-do list of the logged in user including state of the contributions. The service editor supports the coordinator-driven binding protocol as described in Section 5.1.1. In the *element lists* and *element details* panels, an overview of the mashup as well as more information on the contribution are given. In the *mashup document* panel, the contributor can answer the service request through an HTML form.

The collaboration application manager component is implemented as Java Web application, hosted on an Apache Tomcat server. The user interface components are implemented using Google Web Toolkit[19].

---

[19]https://developers.google.com/web-toolkit/ (accessed January 16th, 2013)

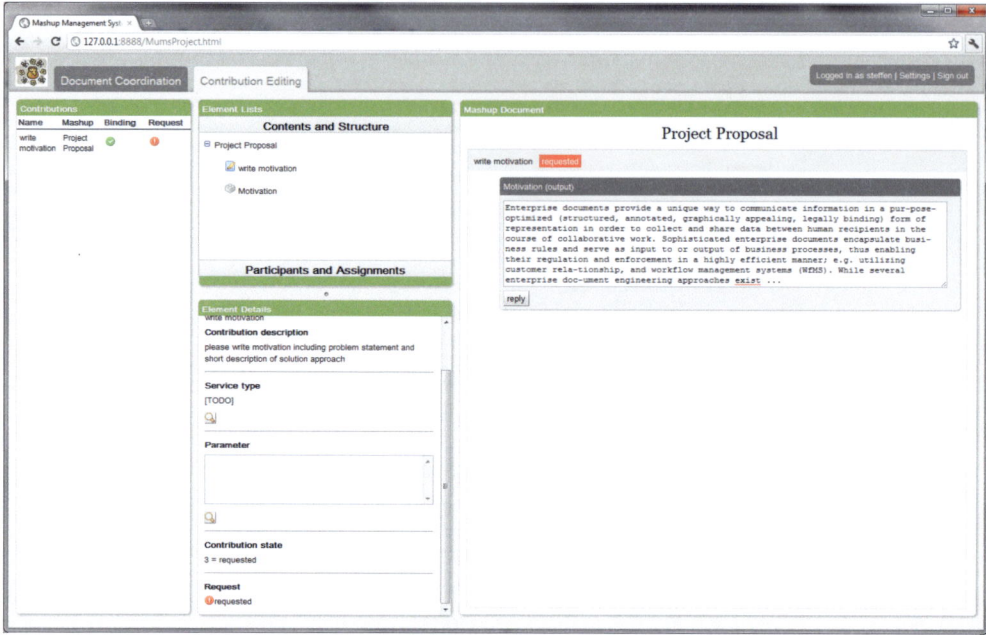

Figure 6.10.: Screenshot of the service editor UI.

The collaboration application exemplifies the utilization of the collaboration infrastructure as regards coordination and human participants. A collaboration, however, might additionally involve software services which require adapters. Exemplary service adapters are described in the following.

6.2.3. Service Adapters

Adapters can be built for software services but also for humans, e.g., as plug-ins to editors or in order to support various communication channels. The adapter framework was used to build three different adapters which are discussed shortly in the following.

- The *e-mail adapter* exemplifies the use of the adapter framework for building communication channels. The e-mail adapter provides a frond end allowing contributors to register as service providers providing their e-mail address. The adapter creates an entry in the mashup registry for the provider. A scheduler of the adapter periodically requests the mashup registry for new contributions the provider is associated with. As soon as a request for contribution is detected, an e-mail is sent to the e-mail address of the provider. The adapter contains an e-mail server which acts as sender of the e-mail. The provider can answer this request using a keyword in the e-mail which is detected by the adapter. The adapter writes the answer into the registry. On receiving a service request, the adapter first retrieves all input results, wraps them into a text and sends this text to the e-mail address of the provider. The provider can again answer with an e-mail, providing the result at a labeled position in the e-mail.

The adapter is built using the Google App Engine[20] which already provides an e-mail server as well as a database to store user data. A large set of features of the adapter framework, e.g., result content retrieval, could be used which made the implementation straightforward.

- The *Web services adapter* serves as proof that Web services can be adapted with automated binding and service response. The adapter requests pictures for a keyword from the flickr API[21]. On deployment, the adapter registers as provider at the mashup registry as well as registers a service type for providing pictures. A scheduler periodically requests the mashup registry for new contributions the provider is associated with. If these contributions are in state "askedForBinding", the binding is automatically accepted by the adapter. A coordinator might now request the service. A request contains a parameter value with a search term which is required by the adapter as well as a result on which the picture should be written. Having requested a picture from the flickr API, the adapter writes the hyperlink of the picture back to the result. Thus, on each request, the adapter potentially returns a different picture. On each request, another keyword can be provided.

  As for the e-mail adapter, several features of the adapter framework were used during implementation, e.g., automated registration and binding.

- The *Web cam adapter* connects a service providing pictures which change frequently. As example Web service the Webcams.travel API [22] was chosen. Changes of the pictures are not under the control of the coordinator. In order to reduce the dependency on the Web service, the adapter caches pictures on the Web. As outlined in Section 6.1.3, media contents like pictures are referenced as hyperlinks in the persistency and need to be stored elsewhere. They are only loaded if the collaboration application requests it. A second feature of the adapter is the ability to set back the picture in the mashup to an older version, for example if the quality or motive of the source changes.

  Accordingly, the adapter is realized with two modes. In the *normal mode*, as soon as the adapter is called by the coordinator service messaging component, it retrieves the most actual picture from the Web cam service, uploads it to Amazon Simple Storage

---

[20]https://developers.google.com/appengine/ (accessed January 16th, 2013)
[21]http://www.flickr.com/services/api/ (accessed January 16th, 2013)
[22]http://de.webcams.travel/developers/ (accessed January 16th, 2013)

Service (S3)[23], and replies the hyperlink of the picture on S3 to the coordinator service messaging. The adapter then starts a scheduler which periodically queries the Web cam service for new versions of the picture. If an update is detected, the update is propagated to the coordinator service messaging. In this mode, the mashup always includes the most actual version of the Web cam picture depending on the chosen scheduler time.

The *stop and setback mode* allows coordinators to choose an older version of the picture stored in S3 and to stop the scheduler. A parameter value sent with the request to the adapter defines the selected picture version.

The three adapters illustrate that during adapter development different requirements as regards coordinator demands or Web service behavior and quality have to be taken into account. A service adapter might provide different access modes for the adapted service. The creation of an adapter thus involves software engineering activities and can not be performed by end users on demand. The creation of adapters, however, is eased with the adapter framework.

6.3. Conclusion and Discussion

The previous sections demonstrate how to realize the collaboration model by means of service-oriented infrastructure technologies including RESTful Web services, complex event processing, and rich Web 2.0 applications. The fundamental parts of the collaboration model are realized as discussed in Table 6.5.

Table 6.5.: Realization of collaboration model components through the collaboration infrastructure.

Collaboration Model Component	Realization
Component model (Section 4.1)	Components are realized as providers exposing a RESTful interface for delivering service instances. Adapters to existing Web services or for human channels can be created using the adapter framework. Providers support atomic activities which return one or more results. A result is either text or a hyperlink. Components can be published and discovered in the mashup registry.

Continued on next page

---

[23]http://aws.amazon.com/de/s3/ (accessed January 16th, 2013)

Table 6.5 – *Continued from previous page*

Collaboration Model Component	Realization
Composition model (Section 4.2)	Result structures including identified required contributions and input/output relations are stored as mashups in the mashup persistency. The infrastructure accepts and stores any content in textual format or a hyperlink as result. If specific formats are required, collaboration applications require renderers to represent the content. Contributions are associated with providers in the mashup registry.
Participation protocol framework (Section 5.1)	The mashup registry stores the contribution state. Providers and coordinators set the state according to binding protocols. Storing the state centrally in the registry allows providers to retrieve personal to-do lists. Service execution protocols are performed by the service messaging component which communicates with providers. Execution is based on navigation through result structures which might result in communication overhead. Results are sent in a response message and stored as values in the persistency rather than as references. While copying contents might produce complex and hardly manageable knowledge bases, it enables to develop variants and improvements of contents suitable to different collaborations. If a service is not available anymore, the contents is still stored in the mashup.
Event model (Section 5.2)	The rule engine architecture enables the definition of event types as classes with attributes. The infrastructure provides basic event types. Developers can, however, add events types as required. Events are input to the rule engine which is able to detect composite events.
Coordination rule mechanism (Section 5.3)	The rule engine supports the creation of rules as well as starting and stopping rule execution for specific mashups. The infrastructure provides one action type for executing service requests. The rule engine, however, is open for additional action types. Sequence and automation rules are evaluated in the infrastructure.

The infrastructure was designed following principles of REST. Services in REST are resources which makes the paradigm artifact-oriented and suitable to represent composite documents. Resources possess a state which can be changed during activities. The composition of stateful resources ideally maps to the composition of result documents created during a number of activities. The usage of REST, however, comes with a number of consequences.

In the presented infrastructure, entities communicate with each other through service interfaces. The communication is an ad hoc dialog between distributed services. Interactions are not planned or prescribed but rather follow standardized interaction protocols. REST principles like HATEOAS and addressability of resources naturally enable this style of communication as no indirection is introduced by using a central instance like a service bus [11]. The interaction protocols, however, are complex and produce overhead as regards communication between provider and coordinator. This complexity is due to enabling asynchronous call-by-value service responses required for human participation as well as enabling access to results via the same service interface in order to enable reusability. Related work as regards RESTful service composition [107][6] realize easier to implement communication protocols. These approaches, however, do not support ad hoc communication between services but modeled composition of resources where interactions are planned in advance. Complexity can be partially managed through (semi-)automating communication and encapsulating communication in adapter logic. For example, all input results are pushed automatically to the provider adapter which offers a user interface.

Standardization of the provider interface results in the fact that already existing services also need to be supported with an adapter implementing the protocols, even those which already come with a REST API. Standardization, however, also enables developers to build service adapters which can be reused in different collaborations. Assuming a community of users and open registries, the adapter framework is one approach to foster a growing set of available service adapters on the Web for different use cases. Using uniform interfaces and media types for protocols thus can help to scale as regards participants in a collaboration as the contract for interaction is clear [141]. Uniform interfaces enable loose coupling between services and coordinator which allows services to evolve without braking the interface and to be more easily replaced. For human participants, adapters can be integrated into software like editors or social network platforms or provided as specialized application for mobile phones. Adapters can be integrated into the favorite working environment of providers. Clients can potentially be multi-tenant providing interaction channels for more than one person.

Service composition helps to increase the *reuse* of services [68]. Since contributions are associated with a collaboration rather than concrete resources, however, reuse of resources is difficult. For example, a particular dataset created by a human participant is delivered through a contribution in a collaboration. If the dataset should be reused in another collaboration, coordinators can not use the same contribution, since the contribution has a state and path according to the first collaboration. The coordinator of the second collaboration has to create a new contribution and request the human, e.g., in the description, to provide the data set. The provider decides how to reuse the resource. For example, the provider could create a service type for the dataset. An adapter could then automatically create a new contribution for each service request with this service type. Since transformation services, e.g., translators, can be represented as providers offering service types, they can be more easily reused. For each use in a collaboration, simply a new contribution is created, e.g., representing the translation with input parameters for a specific collaboration.

Web technologies – in contrary to WS-* technologies and standards – do not natively support enterprise-level *qualities* like reliable messaging, security, or transactions [108]. Desired qualities most often have to be implemented matching specific system requirements. Since quality insurance is not main focus of the collaboration infrastructure, most of these qualities were not realized in the implementation. Accordingly, for example, essentially every participant could access and write result content without being entitled. Messages, e.g., service requests, might get lost before reaching their target or message content might be changed by an intruder. In order to generate a product version of the infrastructure and the adapter framework which is accepted by users, required qualities have to be analyzed and implemented.

As regards related work of the infrastructure, a number of approaches exist adopting REST for the representation of business processes [73][151][117] or process documents [17] in order to support flexibility and Web scalability [128]. The focus of these approaches, however, is not on flexible collaborative document creation. The collaboration application can be seen as domain-specific mashup tool [29] supporting specific types of collaborative document creation. Mashup tools in general allow end users to flexibly compose resources [153]. Existing tools, however, do not focus on support of collaborative composition of resources to facilitate collaborative document creation.

In order to show that the collaboration model and system are applicable to a range of different use cases, two pilot use case demonstrators were developed. The following sections present focus and realization details of the two use cases.

7. Use Case Studies

The proof of concept presented in the previous chapter showed feasibility of the presented collaboration model. In order to demonstrate applicability of the collaboration model and infrastructure to different kinds of collaborative document creation, model and infrastructure were systematically applied to two pilot use cases: participatory service design and community-driven pattern creation. The results are two concrete software architectures and prototypes augmented with different participation protocols, coordination rules, event types, and service types. The use case studies were accomplished in an exploratory, analytical way rather than in an experimental field study. Both studies were performed in cooperation with domain experts in order to get a realistic insight into the applicability of the model.

In the design features of the collaboration model presented in Chapter 3 several assumptions are made, e.g., regarding participating roles, hierarchical documents, or atomic content production activities. The pilot use cases examine the assumptions as summarized in Table 7.1.

Table 7.1.: Aspects for use case studies and their evaluation.

Aspect	Examination
roles (DF 1-1)	Which roles are involved? Are coordinator and contributor roles sufficient for the use case?
participants (DF 1-2)	Which kind of providers are involved – humans and/or software service providers? How does integration of software services benefit the use case?
activities (DF 1-3)	Which activities are performed during collaboration? Are atomic content production activities sufficient?
artifact structure and evolution (DF 2-1)	How is the result document structured? Can the structure be used for the identification of activities?
document model (DF 2-2)	Which document model and formats are required? Is document model independence advantageous?
reuse (DF 2-3)	Are produced document parts reused? Is reuse of results applicable?

Continued on next page

Table 7.1 – *Continued from previous page*

Aspect	Examination
binding protocols (DF 3-1)	How are participants bound to activities? Which binding protocols are instantiated? Is openness as regards participation protocols a desired design feature?
resource and activity states (DF 3-2)	How are activities related to artifact parts? Which execution protocols are instantiated? Is state tracking used?
document access (DF 3-3)	Do participants consume existing document parts?
events (DF 4-1)	Is the event model used or extended? Is the event model including atomic events sufficient?
dependencies and rules (DF 4-2)	Are rules used? Which dependencies are managed through rules? Is the rule model sufficient?

Each of the following Sections 7.1 and 7.2 provides first a short motivation for the studied use case, followed by a detailed description of the collaboration scenario and the instantiation of the collaboration model including implemented participation protocols, event types, and rules. Section 7.3 concludes with a discussion of the use cases as regards the design features.

7.1. Participatory Service Design

Models in software or service engineering serve as communication and discussion media to improve quality of designs as well as allow co-workers to obtain a common view of a product, process, or service. Through modeling, co-workers can improve the understanding of complex aspects using a visual representation. For instance, engineers create different types of models in order to capture important issues of a project, facilitate collaboration and coordination as well as to enable automation of activities [136].

The focus of the use case described in this section is *participatory service design* where service design models are created in a collaborative way. In the examined case of participatory service design, services are considered as primarily non-technical offerings of value-propositions to customers [150]. The use case is published in [149]. The following explanations advance and discuss the results presented in the publication in the context of the collaboration model and system.

Participatory service design allows for the involvement of different stakeholders in the role of service providers and service consumers into the analysis, design, and development of services [55][58]. As an example, stakeholders in service design in the public sector include citizens, municipalities, and corporations. Participation of different stakeholders during the design life cycle promises to better address the interests and needs of all parties involved during design. Accordingly, participation might improve customer satisfaction and adherence to relevant policies and laws [55]. Involving different stakeholders, however, is a complex task [149]. "In service design, stakeholders typically are represented by groups of experts, including software engineers, infrastructure providers, decision-makers, and legal experts. These stakeholders collaborate with each other, contributing specific knowledge. Results of the collaboration are manifested in one or more design artifacts (such as documents or code), which correspondingly address the diversity of relevant service aspects, including technical, business-related, or legal ones. Participatory service design can thus be seen as the process of coordinating a set of stakeholders, where each stakeholder is represented by one or more experts and contributes to the creation of design artifacts" [149].

7.1.1. Instantiation

In order to illustrate participatory service design, the collaboration scenario as well as the service design method chosen for this use case study are outlined in the following. As already several methods and models exist for service design in general, one method is selected to be extended with collaboration features. Subsequently, the instantiation of the collaboration model for participatory service design is described, followed by a short presentation of the prototype implementation.

Collaboration Scenario

The service design method selected for the use case study is *service feature modeling* [150] during which a document called *service feature model (SFM)* is produced. According to the concept described in [149], SFMs are created during a dedicated modeling phase. The result of service feature modeling is a design artifact including multiple design and implementation alternatives for different aspects of a service, e.g., a set of authentication mechanisms which can be used in the implementation of a service. Design and implementation alternatives are captured in a hierarchical structure of *features* and *feature attributes*. During a subsequent configuration phase, experts choose the design alternatives to be realized, e.g., a concrete authentication mechanism, based on requirements and constraints, e.g., that a service has to be delivered electronically. The result of the configuration phase is an artifact representing one single service design.

The creation of one single artifact which contains dedicated parts, i.e., features, including knowledge of different domains makes service feature modeling an ideal candidate for this use case study. The use case study realizes collaborative service feature modeling during the modeling phase where a *service feature diagram* as a graphical representation of an SFM is created. In the collaboration scenario, an organizational unit is in charge of the design of a new service. The organizational unit wishes to involve expertise from other, potentially orthogonal organizational units, e.g., for service features on legal, budget, or compliance, and therefore appoints a coordinator. The coordinator acts as a caretaker who identifies responsibilities and assigns them to individuals as well as supports communication and coordination between participants [111]. During collaboration, diverse participants contribute model parts for different aspects to a single SFM.

An example for collaborative service feature modeling is given in Figure 7.1 where a service is designed to enable employees to access their social security insurance record. Besides the service engineer acting as project coordinator, a legal expert is involved who contributes knowledge in terms of legal and security aspects. A cost estimation service contributes attribute values for electronic and postal record delivery. For a more detailed description on service feature modeling in general the reader is referred to [149][150].

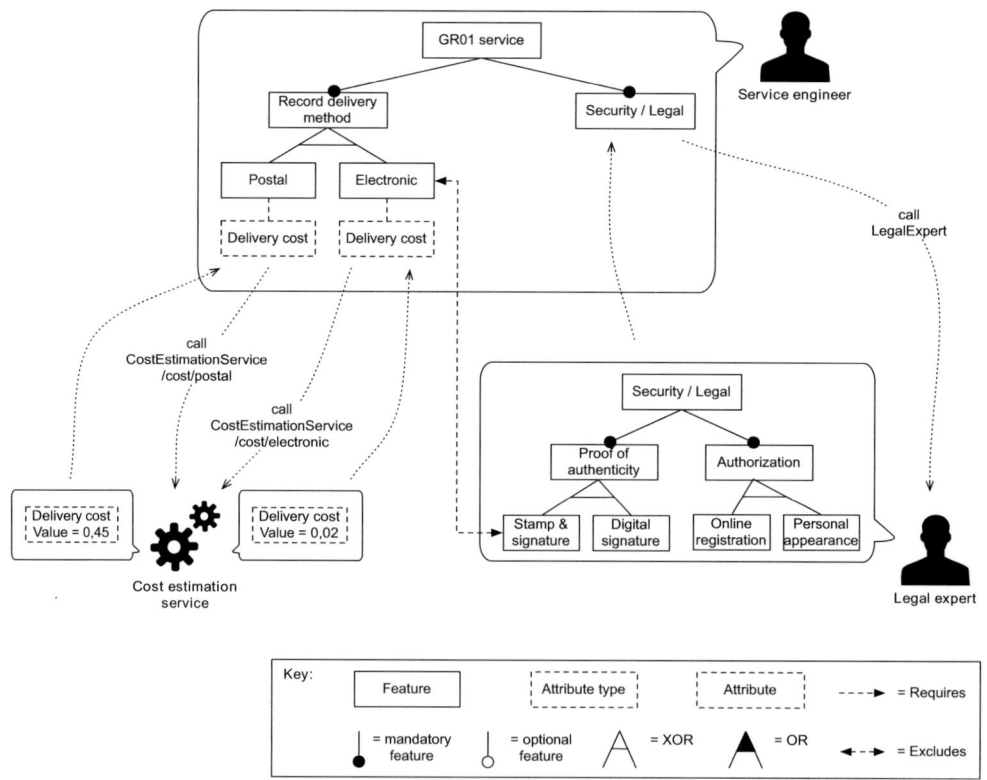

Figure 7.1.: Example of an SFM composed of services (source: [149]).

Application of the Collaboration Model

The component model presented in Section 4.1 is instantiated as follows. Providers are human experts or software services who contribute services to deliver or refine results to be included into the overall SFM. Resource content delivered by services are simple attribute values or complex SFMs including feature trees. Attribute values represent measurable, non-functional characteristics of a feature and are primitive data types [149].

The composition model presented in Section 4.2 is adapted and extended for the instantiation of the overall collaboration model to service feature modeling as shown in Figure 7.2.

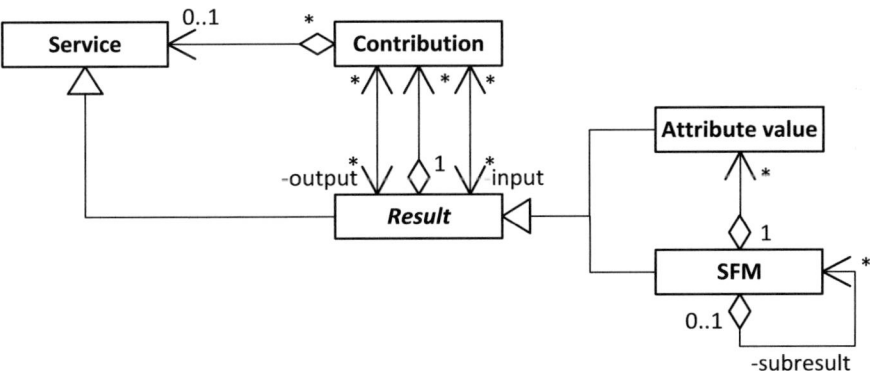

Figure 7.2.: Adapted and extended composition model for collaborative service feature modeling (based on [149]).

Suitable to the resources offered by the providers, the results to be produced and refined during collaboration are either SFMs or attribute values. SFMs might contain subresults. For instance, the overall service in Figure 7.1 is an SFM containing the "security/legal" SFM. As attribute values are simple data types, they cannot be further decomposed.

For service binding in the use case study, the coordinator-initiated binding protocol as presented in Section 5.1.1 is instantiated which enables a top-down collaboration where a coordinator decides on participant selection. The service request/response protocol is used as presented in Section 5.1.2. Accordingly, SFMs are assigned to responsible participants of a collaboration who eventually deliver their results. Activities include creation and revision of results.

During collaboration, several collaboration-specific dependencies exist which are supported using extensions of the event model and the definition of domain-specific rules: (a) cross-tree relationships, (b) attribute type dependencies, and (c) attribute provisioning dependencies.

(a) *Cross-tree relationships.* Cross-tree relationships between features denote that one feature either requires or excludes the existence of another feature in a configuration. For example, a cross-tree relationship exists between the "electronic" record delivery and the "stamp & signature" authentication mechanism denoting that the one excludes the other [149]. In order to avoid inconsistencies caused through changes or deletion of a feature which is part of a cross-tree relationship, the modeler of the affected feature should be informed about changes. Accordingly, the event model described in Section 5.2 is extended with the event types `FeatureUpdated` and `FeatureDeleted` [149] as depicted in Figure 7.3. In addition, a `notify` action is added to the actions of the rule mechanism.

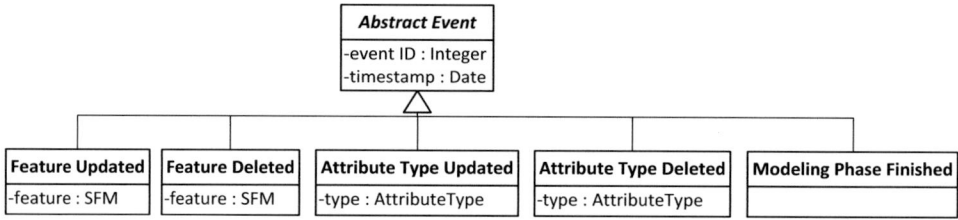

Figure 7.3.: Additional events for collaborative service feature modeling.

Cross-tree relationships originally are defined between features in the document model, the SFM. In order to manage cross-tree relationships through the ECA rule mechanism, they are translated to rules as soon as they are created in the document model, i.e., as soon as a result including a cross-tree relationship is created. As an example, in case the "electronic" delivery is changed to "postal", the relationship becomes obsolete and its author, the legal expert who defined the relationship in the document model, is notified as defined in the following rule (adapted version from [149]). The terms in quotes in the following rules are unique IDs.

```
ON FeatureUpdated(feature="electronic")
       V FeatureDeleted(feature="electronic")
DO notify("legal expert");
```

(b) *Attribute type dependency.* In an SFM, attribute types can be specified to define common characteristics of attributes like the unit for costs in the insurance record example [149]. An attribute might be of a specific type which denotes an attribute type dependency between an attribute and its type. Several attributes might use the same type. Changes of an attribute type can lead to inconsistencies, for instance, if the attribute type "delivery cost" is changed from "Euro / delivered record" to "Euro / month". In such cases, all affected modelers of attributes, in the example the service engineer, need to be informed [149]. Accordingly, the event model is extended with the event types `AttributeTypeUpdated` and `AttributeTypeDeleted` as depicted in Figure 7.3. As soon as an attribute is created in the document model, i.e., a result including an attribute is created, an ECA rule is instantiated. The notified modelers might then request the services delivering the attribute values for updates. The following rule implements this behavior for the described example (adapted version from [149]).

```
ON AttributeTypeUpdated(type="delivery cost")
      ∨ AttributeTypeDeleted(type="delivery cost")
DO notify("service engineer")
```

(c) *Attribute provisioning dependency.* Cross-tree relationships and attribute type dependencies are content dependencies based on the document model used in service feature modeling. A third type of dependency to be managed is the attribute provisioning dependency. Attribute provisioning dependencies are prerequisite relations motivated from a process perspective. Attribute values allow modelers to include real-time data or complex calculations into the model. Such services should be invoked during the configuration phase which succeeds the modeling phase in order to allow participants to decide based on the most actual values [149]. Services might, however, not be able to push updates to the SFM on their own. Therefore, an event of a the newly defined type `ModelingPhaseFinished` is used which denotes the end of the modeling and the beginning of the configuration phase. A project coordinator can emit the event of type `ModelingPhaseFinished` manually, e.g., through an external channel to a modeling tool. The event of type `ModelingPhaseFinished` might trigger a rule which requests all contributions delivering an attribute value. Alternatively, or additionally, a coordinator might specify rules which request those services at a certain point in time, e.g., every morning at 8am. The following rules coordinate both alternatives. Such rules can be defined by human coordinators throughout the collaboration. Alternatively, the rules can automatically be created by the collaboration system as soon as attribute value providers are bound to a contribution and deleted if the binding is removed [149]. The following rule is a slightly adapted version of the rule presented in [149].

```
ON ModelingPhaseFinished
DO requestContribution("benchmark");

ON Timer(*-*-*-08-00)
DO requestContribution("benchmark");
```

The listed dependencies and rules are not claimed to be complete. Rather, the rules are found suitable to avoid inconsistencies during collaborative service feature modeling [149].

Implementation

The prototype system supporting collaborative service feature modeling is designed as shown in Figure 7.4. As part of the *collaboration server*, the *SFM manager* fulfills functionality of the mashup persistency as described in Section 6.1.3. Besides storing results and offering them as services through the model interface, the SFM provides the model integrator which parses SFMs on delivery or update before storing them in the SFM persistency. The model integrator communicates with the coordination engine.

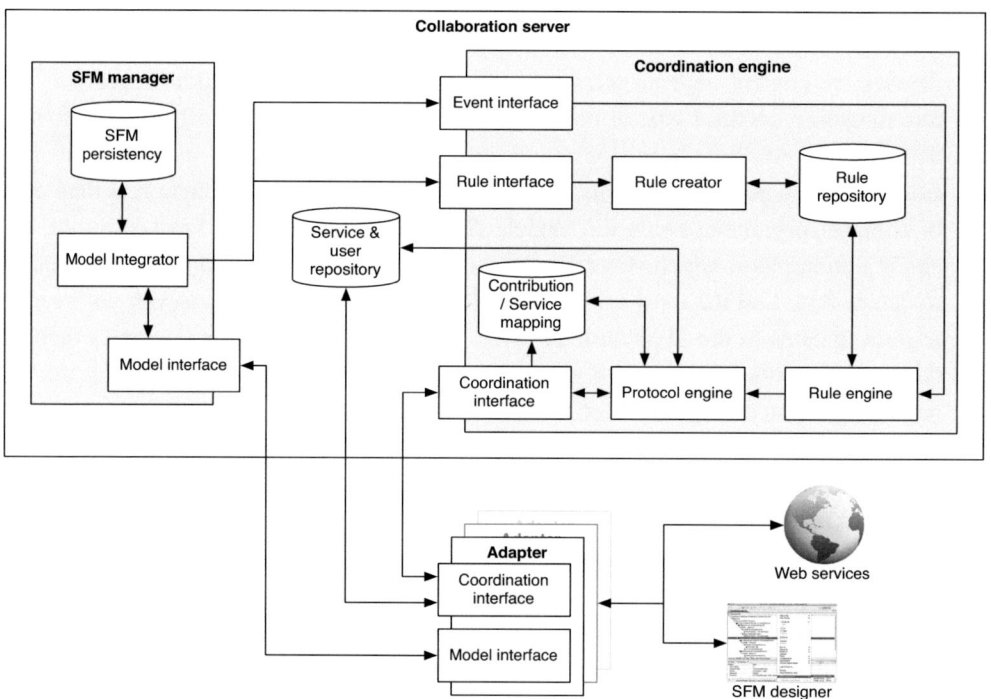

Figure 7.4.: Architecture of a system for collaborative service feature modeling (source: [149]).

The *coordination engine* fulfills the functionalities of the rule engine (Section 6.1.5) and the coordinator service messaging (Section 6.1.4). Accordingly, the coordination engine provides an interface to listen for events and an interface to create rules. For example, as soon the model integrator in the SFM manager detects the update of a feature in an SFM, it sends an event to the coordination engine using the event interface. In addition, the model integrator might automatically create rules using the rule interface, e.g., if it detects a new cross-tree relationship which should be managed automatically. Rules are stored in the rule repository and fed into the rule engine. If the rule engine detects an event pattern, it causes an action, e.g., requests a service. The protocol engine provides the functionality of the coordinator service messaging component described in Section 6.1.4 and manages service calls.

The *service and user repository* in combination with the *contribution/service mapping repository* represents the mashup registry as presented in Section 6.1.2. Accordingly, the service and user repository stores available providers and their capabilities. The contribution/service mapping repository stores contributions and associated concrete services in a separate repository.

Contributors can access the collaboration server using adapters. Adapters include Web services as attribute value providers. In addition, for a user front end with modeling capabilities for SFMs, an adapter is built to the existing Eclipse-based *SFM designer* [149]. The SFM designer adapter enables coordinators to create expected results, and select and associate experts from the service and user repository. The SFM designer adapter also allows service providers to contribute their results.

7.1.2. Discussion and Related Work

The presented use case study demonstrates the application of the collaboration model for the collaborative integration of diverse design issues into a coherent design artifact, an SFM. Parallel work in collaborative modeling can improve efficiency. One of the challenges of collaborative modeling, however, is the integration of sub-model parts which are contributed by participants in parallel into one coherent model [115]. Accordingly, in this use case study, model parts are represented as services which are delegated to experts who can independently contribute to a central uniform design artifact. The application of the collaboration model to participatory service design results in the following findings.

- The use case study exposes a hierarchically organized form of collaboration in a *team of experts*. Participants act in the roles modeler, coordinator, and attribute service provider. Further roles, e.g., specified in a specific role model, are not required in the use case. Human participants are experts which are selected according to responsibilities and knowledge. The coordinator decides whom and how many participants to integrate. Accordingly, the coordinator-driven participation protocols proposed in the collaboration model can be used. While modeling in smaller groups is more efficient and the participation most often is higher, the integration of more experts increases the quality and completeness of the model [115]. Experience on optimal group size for modeling with the presented approach might be gained in field studies. The collaboration model does not delimit the number of participants.

- Modeling SFMs in their graphical notation is a *complex task* mainly performed independently by single responsible persons. Modelers use suitable editors to perform this task. The delivery of the result SFM is a contribution to the collaboratively created central SFM which might have dependencies with other SFMs. The delivery can therefore be represented as an *atomic activity*, and thus, coordination mechanisms can be applied on the activity. No complex, domain-specific activities need to be introduced into the collaboration model. In an atomic activity, an SFM including several features can be contributed. This is realized through separating the document model from the service composition model: Although SFMs include a hierarchy of features, they are not mapped on a result in a one-to-one relationship. Rather, subtrees of an overall SFM are mapped on results. Therefore, the tree structure of the SFM itself does not necessarily correspond to the tree structure of the service composition model. Coordinators can identify complete SFMs representing an aspect of the service design and assign them to an expert for the aspect. The reusability of results is improved since complete modeled aspects can be integrated into the design models of different services. The separation of document and composition model, however, introduces an indirection in the treatment of rules. Relationships in the document model need to be constantly synchronized with the rule base. A specialized software component needs to keep relationships and rules consistent.

- In order to support domain-specific dependencies, a set of simple event types are specified. The *dependency management* mainly focuses on the prevention of inconsistencies in SFMs. Potential domain-specific inconsistencies are detected through rules which are automatically created by a software component. Responsible participants are notified and can resolve possible conflicts. The rules do not resolve inconsistencies because the considered dependencies are content dependencies which can only be resolved by humans understanding the semantics of the model. A large set of rules might be created by participants and automatically by the collaboration system. Future versions of the collaboration application should consider rule management functions adapted to the use case.

- The *integration of software services* is used in two respects. First, modelers are enabled to use their preferred tool, e.g., the SFM designer, to perform the complex task of modeling the SFM they are responsible for. Plug-ins for such tools can be created with the adapter framework. Second, the ability to integrate software services appears to be convenient for the integration of dynamic data or complex calculations into the model. Dynamic data like benchmarks or sensor data can be kept up to date more easily. For each software service, however, a distinct adapter needs to be implemented which might impair usability of the approach.

A similar approach to collaborative service feature modeling is used in [32] where UML models are created by distributed software engineering teams. UML models can be decomposed by software engineers into fine-grained model parts. Model parts can then be modified by distributed participants. As collaborative service feature modeling, this approach enables hierarchical breakdown of models, event-based notifications, and coordination mechanisms for the management of concurrent access and dependencies between model parts [149]. In [154], a model and tool allow SOA architects to collaboratively capture SOA design decisions and their alternatives. Coordination support is provided during the decision phase in the form of dependencies between decisions similar to the cross-tree relationships in service feature modeling. The instantiation is implemented in a wiki and supports textual descriptions in a predefined document model. Both approaches, however, "do not (yet) support assignment of modeling parts through a coordinator to responsible participants and do not enable the integration of contents provided by software services into the models" [149].

To summarize, the use case study focuses on the integration of contents delivered by individual experts into a coherent model as well as the integration of software services. The applied participation protocols reflect a hierarchical, coordinator-driven collaboration. The following use case, on the contrary, targets at an open, community-driven model of collaboration which still implements mechanisms for coordination.

7.2. Community-Driven Pattern Repository

Design *patterns* capture frequently used solutions for common problems in order to communicate those solutions. Pattern descriptions usually are structured uniformly, including the problem description, the description of the solution to the problem, consequences of applying the solution, examples for application as well as dependencies to other patterns. In *pattern repositories* sets of patterns in a certain application domain can be collected using a community-driven, collaborative approach. Plenty of pattern collections exist, addressing various contexts and levels of application. For instance, the authors of [49] present a collection of patterns for reusable solutions in object-oriented software design which serve as blueprints for software developers. The patterns constitute classes as well as relationships or interactions between them.

The focus of the use case study described in the following is a community-driven pattern repository for a specific type of patterns, service network management patterns. The use case study is published in [125]. The following explanations advance and discuss the results presented in the publication in the context of the collaboration model and system.

7.2.1. Instantiation

The following sections introduce service network management patterns and well as describe the pattern repository for such patterns and the instantiation of the collaboration model for this use case.

Collaboration Scenario

Service network management involves activities to design a platform which hosts and offers software applications as services. In particular, platform architects need to realize suitable structures and control mechanisms in order to exploit network effects [125]. For example, successful service platform operators like Salesforce and Netsuite leverage economic network effects to improve their portfolio of offered services on the one hand and grow the customer base on the other hand. The Dynamic Network Notation (DYNO) can be used by platform operators to model platforms as regards their control mechanisms and network effects [124]. As described in [125], *service network management patterns* capture experience of successful and unsuccessful service network management approaches in order to enable platform operators and researchers to learn from and to share knowledge on best practices. Descriptions of service network management patterns are organized according to the structure presented in Table 7.2. The table also introduces the *"communicate the number of subscribed users"* pattern as an example. A detailed description of service network management patterns is provided in [125].

Table 7.2.: Service network management pattern structure and example (based on [125]).

Name	Description
Pattern ID	Unique pattern identifier.
Pattern Name	Meaningful name of the pattern, *e.g., communicate the number of subscribed users pattern*
Version	Version number.
Authors	The authors that contributed to the pattern, followed by the release version in brackets.
Status	Under revision, released.
Pattern Type	Pattern or anti-pattern.

Continued on next page

Table 7.2 – *Continued from previous page*

Name	Description
Intent	Description of the addressed service network management problem. *For example, the "communicate the number of subscribed users" pattern provides a solution for raising network effects that shall be exploited to grow the user base.*
Applicability	Description of the contexts where the pattern can be applied including preconditions.
Solution	Detailed description of the pattern, its accomplishment, limitations, etc. *For example, the "communicate the number of subscribed users" pattern proposes to publish the current number of platform users, thus, apply an informational control mechanism, which motivates new users to register at the platform and consume services.*
Diagram	Graphical representation of the pattern.
Consequences	Description of pros, cons, and limitations.
Sources	If code for parts or all of a pattern can be downloaded at a URI, this URI is included here, accompanied by additional information e.g., license information and deployment guides.
Examples	Real life examples.
Included Patters	Cross reference to included patterns.
Related Patterns	Cross reference to closely related patterns. *For example, a related pattern of the "communicate the number of subscribed users" pattern is the "award a bonus" pattern which applies a motivational control mechanism to enforce growth of the user base. The "consumer-sided network effect" pattern combines a set of patterns for growing the user base.*

When capturing a reusable base of knowledge on service network management in an open pattern repository, platform operators could profit from experience in different market segments. Authors of pattern descriptions could benefit from the continuous advancement of their suggested pattern through the community. Therefore, the knowledge base needs to be open to any user willing to contribute knowledge. This openness, however, comprises the risk of low-quality contributions [125]. As suggested in [125], a pattern repository should therefore enable a community to initiate and evolve individual patterns until they are generally accepted.

The collaboration scenario in this use case study aims to support openness as regards participants and contributions on the one hand and, on the other hand, enable coordination mechanisms to improve quality of contributions. In the collaboration scenario, members of the community create, revise, and approve patterns in the specified, but extensible structure. During collaboration, community members play different roles [125]. Contributors deliver content according to their expertise, e.g., textual descriptions or diagrams, for a pattern. Existing patterns or parts thereof can be reviewed and updated by revisers. Any community member can play these roles. To assure quality of patterns, approvers are required to state that a pattern is valuable and sufficiently described in its current version. An approval can be made at any time throughout the collaboration by any community member. Approvals are performed by service providers in order to avoid bottle necks at the coordinator as well as enable community-based approval.

Each member of the community can create a pattern in the repository. The creator of an initial pattern is appointed as coordinator of this pattern who specifies coordination mechanisms for the pattern [125]. For instance, a coordinator might assure that the author of a solution description is notified whenever an update to a diagram happens. The coordinator might delegate description tasks to certain community members. For instance, the coordinator might assign a revision task to a community member who might be interested in revising.

Application of the Collaboration Model

In order to support the described collaboration scenario, the component model presented in Section 4.1 is instantiated as follows. Providers are human experts who deliver, refine, or approve service network management patterns or parts thereof. Providers produce text or figures as result resource content. Results might be delivered through various channels, for instance, e-mail, a DYNO editor, or a Web front end. In addition, an ID generator can be used to create unique pattern IDs. Adapters to services from the Web might provide example texts or connect source code repositories.

The composition model presented in Section 4.2 is extended as shown in Figure 7.5. The results to be composed are descriptions of patterns including diagrams and text. Important contributions for service network management patterns are the provisioning of parts of the pattern description (e.g., pattern ID, intent, solution) through contributors, the revision of these parts through revisers, and the approval of a pattern document through approvers.

As regards binding protocols, the pattern repository is configured with the self-service binding protocol as well as the coordinator-initiated binding protocol as presented in Section 5.1.1. On the one hand, interested and committed community members can ask the coordinator for binding to a contribution they want to provision. On the other hand, coordinators still might invite specific service providers, e.g., for approving or revising a suggested pattern [125].

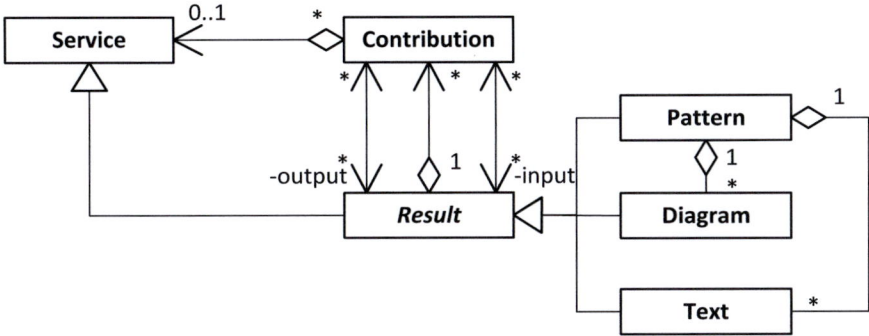

Figure 7.5.: Extended composition model for the pattern repository (based on [125]).

As an example, Figure 7.6 shows parts of the "communicate the number of subscribed users" pattern as composition of results, contributions, and services. In this figure, the pattern contains a pattern ID provided by a software service, a description of the pattern intent written by a human participant, examples retrieved from Web sites, as well as a diagram modeled in DYNO. In addition, the pattern has review, approve, and publish contributions.

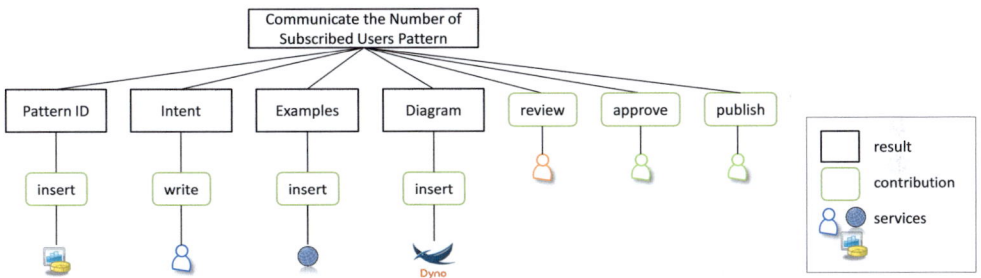

Figure 7.6.: Example service network pattern composed of services (based on [125]).

The execution of services is managed through different request/response protocols for different result types. Pattern results, i.e., root nodes of the result tree, can be identified, approved by a number of services with type approval as well as released as shown in Figure 7.7(a). The transition to state "released" is performed by the coordinator, supported by rules as shown later in the section. The state "released" denotes an agreement of the community on the quality of the pattern. Once in state "released", no changes or approvals can be made to the pattern or any of the subresults.

The transition from state "approved" to "identified" is performed automatically through a rule as any subresult of the pattern is added or updated, for example service A updates

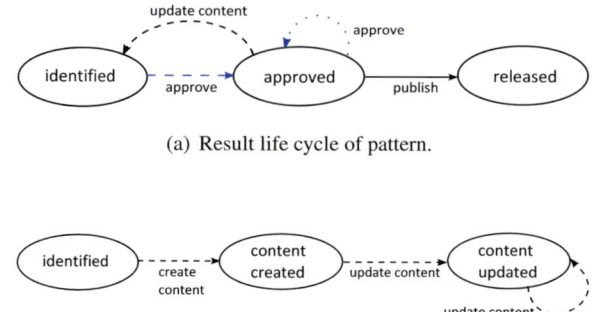

(a) Result life cycle of pattern.

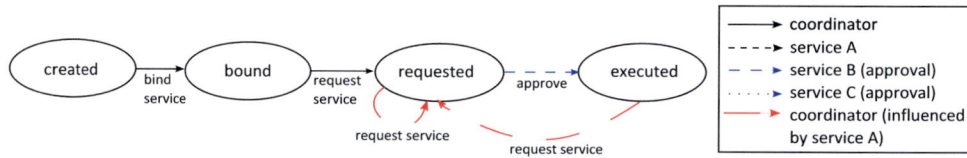

(b) Result life cycle of text or diagram as subresult of pattern.

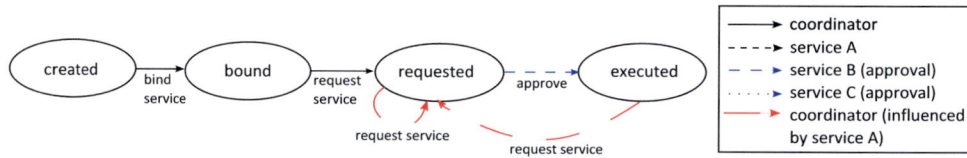

(c) Contribution life cycle of approval.

Figure 7.7.: Service execution protocol.

the subresult in Figure 7.7(b). The contribution life cycle of an approval is presented in Figure 7.7(c) which is associated with service B of type approval. An approval can only be executed on request of the coordinator. If a pattern is transferred from state "approved" to "identified", the approval is requested again in order to proof that the pattern is still valid.

As shown in Figure 7.7(b), all text and diagram results follow the standard service request/response protocol presented in Section 5.1.

The rule mechanism described in Section 5.3 is used in the pattern repository to (a) semi-automate service binding and request/response protocols and (b) manage collaboration-specific dependencies [125].

(a) *Semi-automation of participation protocols.* The protocols involve several coordinator activities which are automated by the coordination engine through the definition of generic, globally defined rules in the repository. Full automation of participation protocols can not be supported by the rules since participating providers potentially perform their contributions manually. The first generic rule enables the automated acceptance of service requests from providers. All binding requests from providers should be accepted by default. Thus, the new event type BindingRequested is defined. Whenever

a provider asks for binding according to the service binding protocol, an event of type
`BindingRequested` is emitted. On every occurrence of such an event, if the contribution is not already bound (the state "bound" is assumed to have the integer value 2 in the rule), the requested binding is automatically accepted by the rule, i.e., the requesting service is bound to the requested contribution. The automated acceptance is instantiated through the following generic rule (adapted version of the rule presented in [125]).

```
ON BindingRequested
IF BindingRequested.contribution.contributionState!=2
DO acceptBinding(BindingRequested.service,
    BindingRequested.contribution)
```

The action `acceptBinding` is an extension to the actions of the rule mechanism which communicates with the registry to set the state of the contribution. As the `acceptBinding` action also changes state, an event is emitted denoting that the contribution is bound [125]. The following generic rule is executed as soon as an event of type Bound is detected and automatically triggers a service request of the bound service. In the example, the bound contributor is requested to write the solution section of the pattern. The rule is an adapted version of the rule presented in [125].

```
ON Bound
DO requestContribution(Bound.contribution)
```

(b) *Collaboration-specific dependency management.* The rule mechanism allows coordinators to define rules for managing dependencies in specific patterns. In the following, rules for managing content dependencies and approval processes are presented. Pattern coordinators should add those rules to the rule engine for their pattern. "In order to allow for comparable quality and design methodology of all patterns in a repository, a repository might provide a template instantiating these rules which can be used for the creation of a new pattern. This template should be combined with a template for structuring patterns" [125]. Still, a coordinator might define additional, individual rules.

During collaboration, *content dependencies* exist between parts such that updates of parts of a pattern might cause inconsistencies in other parts. A content dependency exists for example between a solution and a diagram section of a pattern. In case a diagram is updated, the solution section has to be checked for up-to-dateness; if the solution section is updated, the diagram section has to be checked. The following rules request the contribution for revising the solution section if the diagram is updated and the contribution for revising the diagram if the solution section is updated [125]. The terms in quotes denote unique IDs of results or contributions. The rules are adapted versions of the rules presented in [125].

```
ON ContentCreatedOrUpdated(result="diagram")
DO requestContribution("solutionRevision")

ON ContentCreatedOrUpdated(result="solution")
DO requestContribution("diagramRevision")
```

The rule mechanism helps participants in identifying potential semantic inconsistencies in pattern contents. The participants are in charge of resolving inconsistencies.

In order to allow coordinators to officially declare a pattern as accepted by the community, the collaboration scenario envisages a *pattern approval process*. In an initial setting, three participants need to approve a pattern such that the pattern can be transferred in state "released". Appointing three approvers is assumption-based and subject to optimization in future work [125]. Until approved, the pattern state is under revision. In the collaboration scenario, as soon as a pattern is released, it is published on a Web site. In order to implement the approval process, a rule listens on events of type `ContentApproved` which are emitted as soon as a service of type approval updates a pattern. If three events of type `ContentApproved` are detected one after the other without a content update of any section in the pattern in between, the action requests the contribution for publishing the pattern. The following rule is an adapted version of the rule presented in [125].

```
ON ContentApproved
    → (ContentApproved ∧ ¬ ContentCreatedOrUpdated)
    → (ContentApproved ∧ ¬ ContentCreatedOrUpdated)
DO requestContribution("publish")
```

The presented rule automates the transition of a pattern state from "approved" to "released" as defined in the service execution protocols in Figure 7.7. Coordinators can configure individual rules for automating this transition.

Implementation

For the implementation of the pattern repository, the collaboration infrastructure and application presented in Chapter 6 is adapted to the required protocols. The collaboration application could be used as front end. A screenshot of the front end is shown in Figure 7.8.

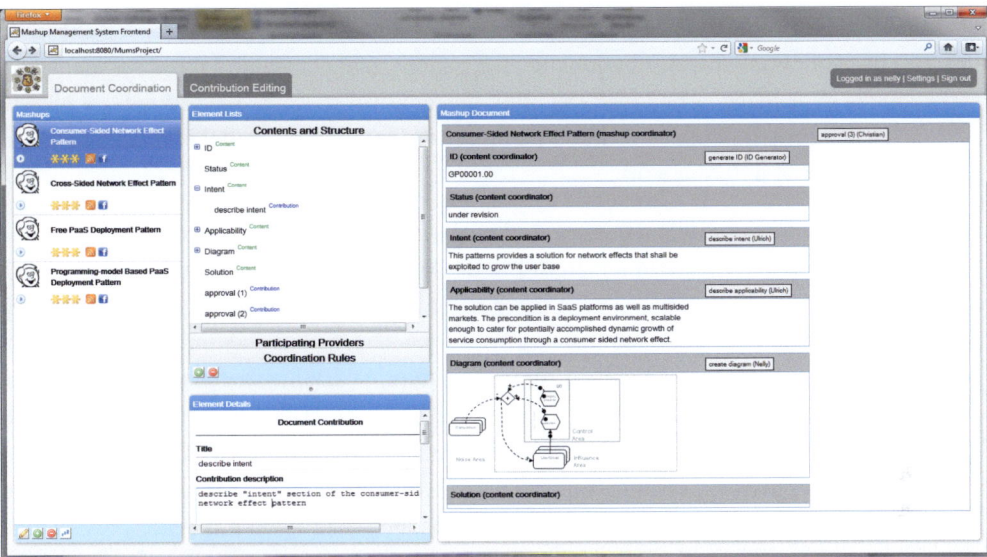

Figure 7.8.: Coordination view of a pattern in the demonstrator showing the "consumer-sided network effect pattern".

7.2.2. Discussion and Related Work

In the presented use case study the collaboration model is instantiated for the creation of service network management patterns in a community-based pattern repository. Pattern repositories in general allow for the aggregation of experience as they are open to communities of practice such that everybody can contribute. Studies in the field of online content production in wikis have shown that also in open communities participants coordinate in order to improve quality of produced content or manage conflicts [69]. Popular coordination mechanisms in this field are discussions about documents as well as the leadership of a few participants who control contributions to documents. Accordingly, the use case study presents a pattern repository which aims to be open for contributions but also involves coordination mechanisms like notifications or an approval process with the goal to assure quality of individual patterns as well as of the repository as a whole. Still, discussion about particular patterns in order to coordinate pattern evolution is not realized in the use case study. The application of the collaboration model to the case of a community-driven pattern repository results in the following findings.

- The use case study envisages a coordinator for each pattern who identifies results and rules for the pattern. The manual coordination overhead can be reduced through providing a pattern *template* at pattern creation time. The template ideally includes (a) the initial pattern structure as presented in Table 7.2 as a result tree, (b) an agreed-upon number of approval contributions for the pattern, and (c) generic rules for managing content dependencies and implementing the approval process. Accordingly, a generic approach for templates in order to automate the creation of expected results needs to be considered in future work.

- In contrary to the result structure in the use case study for participatory service design, the result structure of a pattern is a flat list with one root node where each result represents a section of the pattern description. The result structure is used to identify required content delivery and revision tasks for each text and diagram section. In addition, approval tasks are identified for each pattern. A contributor potentially provides all sections or a large subset of sections for a pattern at the same time. A suitable collaboration application thus should provide an *integrated editor* which allows contributors to provide a set of contributions at once. In addition, a future version of the collaboration application should support automated binding to a specific provider for all sections of a pattern with only one binding request.

- The design of the pattern repository involves *complex design decisions*. For example, the approval process is distributed over several collaboration model parts. First, a pattern is associated with a number of approval contributions associated with services of type approval which update the pattern resource. Second, the pattern follows a newly defined service request/response protocol. Third, rules manage the approval process through semi-automating participation protocols. Additional suitable designs of the approval process might exist. During design of a coordination mechanism, the different nature of the collaboration model components have to be considered. For example, protocols are standardized for all coordinators in a collaboration system. Protocols might be implemented using globally defined rules or a protocol engine. Changes of protocols affect all coordinators in the collaboration system. Collaboration-specific rules affect a particular pattern and allow coordinators to define individual coordination mechanisms. In the use case study, one design decision is to provide the general ability to approve a pattern before it can be released through a protocol. The number of required approvals can be flexibly defined by a coordinator through collaboration-specific rules.

- Contributors can use different *channels* to provide a service, e.g., use their favorite text editor. In addition, an adapter for the DYNO editor could allow participants to update pattern diagrams directly in the appropriate editor and submitting from the editor to patterns. The results might be delivered by the participants in any format. In order to ensure uniformity as regards representation of patterns, however, guidance or a mechanism to ensure format conformity should be introduced in future versions of the infrastructure.

A number of online pattern repositories in various contexts exist. In addition, the concept of exchanging ideas on patterns in a collaborative knowledge base is not new. For instance, the Portland Pattern Repository (PPR)[24], a repository for patterns in software development, came with the first wiki which allowed programmers to easily exchange and edit software design pattern ideas and information. The PPR, however, does not come with structuring or approval functionality [125]. In [91], an interactive pattern repository for inter-organizational business processes is described which allows for a steadily growing pattern base. The authors "define an extensive pattern meta-model, including classes for pattern descriptions with visualizations and relationships between patterns" [125]. Similar to the use case study presented in this section, roles and a pattern review process are defined where a defined number of community members need to accept the pattern. The authors of [91], however, do not describe community-driven collaborative authoring of patterns, integration of external services, e.g., from software systems or the Web, as well as support of channels for participants [125]. Web- or groupware-based approaches for collaborative management of architectural knowledge artifacts like patterns, e.g., [8][155], are well suited for informed decision making during design. These approaches, however, do not allow for the integration of external sources, do not form a community-driven approval process, or support flexible coordination of artifact dependencies [125].

To summarize, the use case study focuses on the community-driven contribution of contents to a service network management pattern repository – reflected by the applied and automated participation protocols – while implementing coordination means towards quality assurance of patterns like an approval process. The instantiation, however, exposes shortcomings as regards usability. For example, the potential complexity of rules to be added might reduce usability and efficiency of pattern creation. Future work should therefore address the implementation of a template mechanism supporting automated instantiation of rules.

7.3. Conclusion and Discussion

The use case studies show feasibility of the design features captured in Chapter 3 as well as demonstrate applicability of the collaboration model to different collaboration scenarios with different coordination requirements. Table 7.3 summarizes the conclusions drawn from the use case studies.

---

[24]http://c2.com/ppr/ (accessed January 22nd, 2013)

Table 7.3.: Summary of use case studies.

Participatory Service Design	Community-driven Pattern Repository	Conclusion
Roles (DF 1-1): Which roles are involved? Are coordinator and contributor roles sufficient for the use case?		
coordinator, modeler, attribute value provider	coordinator, content creator, content reviser, approver	The separation into coordinator and contributor roles are sufficient in both use case studies. While the coordinator role is required in participatory service design, the separation of roles might be needless in the pattern repository since every participant might take any role.
Participants (DF 1-2): Which kind of providers are involved – humans and/or software service providers? How does integration of software services benefit the use case?		
humans and software service providers	mainly humans through different channels, potentially software service providers	The integration of software services is useful in participatory service design, whereas the support of multiple channels enabled through service-orientation is considered useful during the creation of patterns.
Activities (DF 1-3): Which activities are performed during collaboration? Are atomic content production activities sufficient?		
coordination, content creation, review	coordination, content creation, review, approval, publication	For the studied use cases, different types of atomic content production activities as defined in the collaboration model are sufficient.

Continued on next page

Table 7.3 – *Continued from previous page*

Participatory Service Design	Community-driven Pattern Repository	Conclusion
Artifact structure and evolution (DF 2-1): How is the result document structured? Can the structure be used for the identification of activities?		
complete SFMs are used to identify activities	activities are identified per pattern part	The identification of activities can be performed based on the document structure in both use case studies. The mapping of the document model and the required activities, however, has to be deliberated for each use case as it might not be possible to map one-to-one.
Document model (DF 2-2): Which document model and formats are required? Is document model independence advantageous?		
SFMs (complex, hierarchical models), attribute values (simple types)	text, diagrams in a predefined, yet extensible flat structure	The use case studies expose different document models which can be both mapped to a hierarchical structure. The document models include heterogeneous contents, e.g., text, models, or figures. Document model independence therefore is a suitable design feature of the collaboration model.
Reuse (DF 2-3): Are produced document parts reused? Is reuse of results applicable?		
reuse of complete SFMs desired in different service design projects	composition/reuse of complete patterns in other patterns desired	In both use cases, the reuse of larger compositions is desired rather than reuse of atomic document parts. In order to better support reuse of a desired subset of all results, suitable knowledge management mechanisms, e.g., search, should be developed in future work.

Continued on next page

Table 7.3 – *Continued from previous page*

Participatory Service Design	Community-driven Pattern Repository	Conclusion
Binding protocols (DF 3-1): How are participants bound to activities? Which binding protocols are instantiated? Is openness as regards participation protocols a desired design feature?		
participation is driven by co-ordinator, i.e., coordinator-initiated protocols are used	self-service protocols are used in addition to coordinator-initiated protocols	The use cases instantiate different participation protocols in order to support different characteristics of coordination. Therefore, openness as regards binding protocols can be considered an adequate design feature.
Resource and activity states (DF 3-2): How are activities related to artifact parts? Which execution protocols are instantiated? Is state tracking used?		
standard execution protocols and states used; state tracking can be used as coordination mechanism to manage service design project	additional pattern states and protocols; state tracking might inform coordinators of open contributions	Different execution protocols are instantiated, making openness as regards execution protocols an adequate design feature. State tracking might be useful for coordinators in both cases. Suitable UIs are required.
Document access (DF 3-3): Do participants consume existing document parts?		
access to existing parts not necessarily required by modelers	participants require access to existing pattern description parts in order to keep the pattern description consistent	Access to document parts is required in at least one use case study in order to keep the overall document consistent.

Continued on next page

Table 7.3 – *Continued from previous page*

Participatory Service Design	Community-driven Pattern Repository	Conclusion
Events (DF 4-1): Is the event model used or extended? Is the event model including atomic events sufficient?		
additional collaboration-specific atomic events	no additional events	In both use case studies, atomic events are sufficient input for the specified rules. The ability to create new event types is required in one use case study.
Dependencies and rules (DF 4-2): Are rules used? Which dependencies are managed through rules? Is the rule model sufficient?		
collaboration-specific rules add value in that they inform about potential inconsistencies	rules for semi-automation and management of content dependencies and approval processes	The rule model is used in both use case studies to create adequate rules for different purposes.

The use case studies represent instantiations of the collaboration model in order to proof general applicability to different types of collaboration. Although the use case studies only provide first insights into the suitability of the collaboration model for the collaboration scenarios, they still show strengths and weaknesses of the service-oriented collaboration model for different scenarios.

In addition to the results summarized in Table 7.3, the use case studies showed that the collaboration model can be tailored to support different collaboration scenarios with different coordination requirements. The main differences of the use cases are listed in the following.

- The studies differ in the *organization of participants*. Participatory service design involves a number of experts in an organization who are well known to the team. In addition, software services might participate. Contributions, however, are assumed to be controlled by coordinators. A community-driven repository potentially involves persons which do not necessarily know each other. As a result the quality of contributions might differ which results in approval processes realized in the community-pattern repository. Still, participation protocols for both use cases could be implemented.

- The documents created during collaboration differ as regards their *document model*. In participatory service design, complex hierarchical models are composed. In the community-driven pattern repository, a pattern contains a flat list of text and figures. Still, the integration of results into one document could be realized in both use cases since both could be mapped to the hierarchical result structure.

- *Communication and desired degree of automation* differs for both use cases as a result of the different organization of participants. In participatory service design, communication is coordinator-driven and automation of participation protocols is a non-desired feature. Coordinators wish to select the participants and to keep control on the contributions of the participants. In the community-driven pattern repository, anyone can contribute. Accordingly, also self-service binding is allowed. Semi-automation is essential in the pattern repository to reduce manual effort of coordinators as well as allow for open participation. Still, complete automation is not desired, since humans contribute content manually. Both communication and automation requirements could be supported through the participation protocol framework and rules.

- *Coordination requirements* for participatory service design address the avoidance of inconsistencies in the models which is complex as interdependencies are contained inside the model. Service models potentially grow large. Therefore, management of dependencies inside the model is considered an important coordination mechanism. Although the patterns expose a less complex content structure, the pattern repository also supports notification of participants on potential inconsistencies. The focus, however, is on the approval process which is an approach towards quality-insurance of contents. In both cases, the coordination requirements could be realized through rules.

In order to enable adaptability, the collaboration model defines components which can be extended or adapted to the specific needs of a use case. This concept borrows from the *hot spot* concept in object-oriented framework design where hot spots are variation points in frameworks [113]. The hot spots in the collaboration model allow collaboration system providers to add service types, results, event types, or action types. In addition, collaboration-specific service binding and execution protocols can be defined. The collaboration system provider can configure the collaboration system with generic rules. Finally, adapters for different communication channels can be developed exposing service interfaces and encapsulating service interactions. For all of these collaboration model components, a standard solution is provided which can be reused.

Besides collaboration system providers, coordinators might tailor the collaboration system to their needs through specifying collaboration-specific rules. This customization can be performed after initial design of the collaboration system or even during use of the system during collaboration.

The hot spots are accompanied by a set of *prescribed* collaboration model parts. The component model specifies uniform interfaces for services and providers. The composition model prescribes result and contribution interfaces. In addition, the distinction between co-ordinator and contributor roles is prescribed. Although collaboration system providers might add protocols, particular states in these protocols are prescribed by the participation protocol framework. The rule mechanism defines that only ECA rules might be specified.

In both use case studies, the intended collaboration scenarios could be realized with these standardized components. Several prescribed components, however, provide a suboptimal solution. For example, in both use case studies, notifications are used to inform human participants about potential inconsistencies. Notification denotes a unidirectional communication whereas the interaction of services using the request/response protocol is bidirectional. Future work should therefore address protocols and protocol framework extensions for additional communication mechanisms like publish/subscribe.

A number of models and prototypes for cooperative work exist in the research fields of human-computer interaction (HCI) and CSCW which can be tailored. The authors of [37] study collaboration during tailoring of the individual software environment or shared infrastructures for organizations, e.g., helping out or sharing use experiences. An approach for composing cooperative work tools from a small set of existing components is presented in [85]. The authors of [88] discuss the possibilities to enable end-user tailoring: (a) customization, i.e., selecting from predefined configuration options, (b) integration, i.e., adding new functionality through linking predefined components, and (c) extension, i.e., implementing new functionality at given extension points. The mentioned solutions aim to enable end-users or organizations to adapt their working environment to their needs. In contrary to end-user tailoring, the reason for adaptability of the collaboration model in this thesis is to enable the support of different collaboration use cases indicating that coordinating service composition is a suitable mechanism to support flexible collaborative document creation.

Besides demonstrating adaptability, the use case studies show that collaboration system providers need to go through a requirement analysis and design phase. A collaboration system is a software application which has to be carefully designed. The collaboration model should be supplemented with design guidelines, e.g., for the realization of particular coordination mechanisms like an approval process. Relevant design decisions might be examined through the execution of additional use case studies. Having predefined components at hand, however, the initial design of collaboration systems is straightforward and realizable in a short amount of time.

Having discussed the evaluation in which the collaboration model and architecture are applied to select use cases, the following chapters summarize the contributions of this thesis as well as present directions for future work.

Part IV.

Conclusion

8. Summary

The research described in this thesis examines coordination of service compositions in support of human collaboration. The presented solution is based on the hypothesis that the mapping of collaborative document creation on a service composition model enables the integration of human-based and software services into collaborations as well as the coordination of collaborations through mechanisms adapted to the needs of the participants. Reasons and motivation for this hypothesis origin in the state of the art as regards service composition, human collaboration, and coordination presented in Chapter 2. Current service composition approaches, however, suit to support well-structured collaboration but do not facilitate flexible coordination of collaborative document creation.

Collaborative document creation is a complex case as it involves activities performed by different human and non-human providers and the integration of heterogeneous content from different sources. Participants have different experiences and demands as regards the collaboration tool or channel. Often, activities, participants, and required contents can not be defined completely in advance. Still, interdependencies between activities require coordination. In addition, collaboration processes usually are unique and not repeatable as each collaboration follows a different purpose.

In order to address this complexity while still supporting a large number of use cases, this thesis proposes a collaboration model which addresses (a) the integration of human and non-human sources and participants into the same collaboration, (b) a service composition style allowing compositions of resources and activities to flexibly evolve over time, and (c) the ability to coordinate service compositions for different use cases of collaborative document creation throughout their life cycles. The collaboration model consists of five model parts which are uniquely combined to address these challenges as summarized in the following. The model parts can be tailored by collaboration system providers to support specific use cases as well as to design collaboration systems which balance flexibility and control for participants of a collaboration.

- The *component model* presented in Section 4.1 maps contributions provided by human and non-human participants on a service-oriented model and represents participants and their activities using a uniform interface. Existing solutions for the integration of human services into service compositions focus on the adequate representation of service capabilities and require a specification of the service interface through service providers. Models and tools using a uniform representation for all composed entities, e.g., Yahoo!Pipes[25], focus on software services only. The component model represents resources as managed output of services which can be retrieved on request and, thus, allows for the representation of content production or transformation activities. The uniform interface enables easier replacement of services as well as faster creation of human-based services, since less design decisions are required and humans do not have to create a interface specification. The low complexity of the interface with only few methods potentially eases integration of services through humans. Humans might decide to integrate software services to automate certain activities during collaboration, e.g., gathering of sensor data, analytical processing of data, or calculations – summarized as information analysis and acquisition automation [105]. The decision which steps to automate depends on factors like mental workload which might be decreased through automation, skill degradation through delegating work, or reliability of the service [105]. The decision therefore has to be made from case to case. A shortcoming of the component model is that potentially not all activities required during collaboration can be mapped on the interface. Adapters are required for existing services. Both aspects restrict openness of the solution regarding contributors.

The component model can be adapted by collaboration system providers through specialization of the service type taxonomy. Specialization might enable participants to perform collaboration specific search for services or to realize rules based on specific services types, e.g., for approval. In addition, collaboration system providers might develop adapters, e.g., for specific communication channels. The model enables flexibility for participants in a collaboration as it supports human as well as non-human providers. The activities, however, are prescribed to content production activities as well as the methods of the uniform interface.

- Based on the service-oriented component model, the *composition model* presented in Section 4.2 introduces a novel service composition style allowing participants to flexibly evolve and coordinate resource and activity compositions. Existing service composition models focus on the coordination during the execution phase of service compositions and often require too early specification of aspects like service binding. The composition can be performed based on the decomposition of a collaboration goal into required results and the association to contributions of service providers. Such, the composition enables the intuitive coordination of human collaboration through division of labor reducing shared resource dependencies. Using the composition model, coordinators may bind and execute services during all phases of a collaboration. Thus,

---
[25]http://pipes.yahoo.com/pipes/ (accessed June 19th, 2012)

the collaboration model does not distinguish design and execution time. The composition model is independent of the document model as long as the model can be mapped on the hierarchical structure of results. Document parts, however, might be accessed by an arbitrary number of participants at the same time which might result in conflicts and inconsistencies. Concurrency mechanisms need to be applied in order to avoid inconsistencies of shared resources. The composition model is restricted to an asynchronous collaboration model.

As regards adaptation of the composition model, collaboration system providers can specialize result types. In the composition model, the task order is open, allowing coordinators to flexibly evolve the document structure and the required tasks during collaboration. An open number of services can be requested and performed at any time. This flexibility is restricted through the method for structuring a document using a prescribed set of few high-level abstractions – results, contributions, and services. Following this method produces a certain kind of hierarchically structured documents which does not suit all but many creative collaborations.

- The coordination of interactions between participants, i.e., service providers and coordinators, is enabled through the *participation protocol framework* presented in Section 5.1. Using the framework, protocols for service binding and execution can be created which support the integration of human and non-human participants alike. Existing protocol frameworks enable complex interactions of several participants, however, do not focus on the communication between humans and software services. The participation protocol framework already comes with a set of protocols. Additional protocols can be easily specified using the extension points of the framework. As all participants need to follow the specified protocols, automation of protocols is possible. Similar to the automation of information acquisition and analysis through the integration of non-human participants, the decision to automate protocols – which is an automation of action implementation [105] – has to be decided from case to case based on considerations of risks and costs of the automation [105]. In addition, automation can be implemented on different degrees, e.g., automate a single transition in a protocol. The framework does not facilitate complex interactions between more than two participants. Interactions between contributors without coordinator is not supported. As non-human participants are assumed to perform simple content delivery tasks, the communication with them can be mapped on simple protocols. Contrary, the simple protocols enable non-human participation in the first place. These simple protocols, however, do not represent the complexity of human communication protocols. Complex interactions between human participants, e.g., discussions or negotiations, have to be performed outside the system.

As regards adaptation of the participation protocol framework, collaboration system providers can define protocols which start and end with a state specified by the framework. The protocols in the collaboration system then control the execution of communication between participants. The collaboration system providers decide on the degree of flexibility of the participants, e.g., through defining several protocols participants can choose from.

- On top of the composition model and participation protocols, the *event model* (Section 5.2) and the *coordination rule mechanism* (Section 5.3) define a solution to enable flexible coordination of different use cases of collaborative document creation. Existing solutions in service compositions focus on the coordination of repeatable processes. Groupware systems support coordination of humans, but do not explicitly facilitate integration of non-human participants. In addition, they do not focus on providing collaboration-specific coordination means. All activities performed during service composition potentially result in an event which is input to ECA rules. In addition, events stemming from external systems might be integrated. Coordinators can specify ECA rules for different coordination mechanisms like reactions to changes in the composition, detection of potential inconsistencies of shared resources in a document, approval processes based on the flow of service executions, or automation of participation protocols. As has been shown in the use case studies, different degrees of automation can be reached through rules, depending on the requirements of the application. In general, humans are familiar with thinking in ECA rules, e.g., for knowledge representation. At the same time rules allow for formal representation of knowledge in systems [12, p. 73]. The complexity of rule representation as well as the potentially large number of rules to be managed, however, might decrease usability. In addition, verification, e.g., as regards organizational regulations, and traceability within a collaboration are complicated.

  Collaboration system providers can adapt the event model and coordination rule mechanism through the specification of additional event and activity types. In addition, they might define rules which are applied to all collaborations in the collaboration system, e.g., for automation of protocols. Participants might specify any ECA rule suitable to their coordination requirements. They are, however, constrained to the available action and event types and their attributes.

In order to examine the feasibility of the solution, one variant of the collaboration model is realized in an infrastructure and collaboration application as presented in Chapter 6. The realization partially implements REST principles like uniform interfaces for services to be integrated and HATEOAS for communication of produced content, assignment of document parts to responsible participants, or navigation through existing documents. The collaboration application allows humans to create and evolve service compositions through a GUI, thus, hiding service interfaces and protocol logic. While REST suits to realize services and artifact-oriented service compositions, qualities like security or reliability have to be designed and implemented for a product solution. Realization of the protocols using REST principles causes communication overhead which has to be encapsulated in front ends and adapters.

Two use case studies – participatory service design and community-driven pattern repository – are presented in Chapter 7. The use case studies show that tailoring of model and infrastructure to different use cases through collaboration system providers are feasible. Potential advantages through the service-oriented approach include the integration of data sources and the tool environment of users. The complexity of collaborative document creation, however, requires an elaborate analysis and design phase for collaboration systems.

The aspects discussed previously result in a number of future research directions to advance the contributions in future work. These directions are described in the following chapter.

9. Future Research

The research described in this thesis can be developed in different directions including evolution and optimization of the contributions presented in this thesis as well as complementary research directions. A number of potential future work activities, mainly targeting optimization of the contributions, is outlined in the discussion and conclusion sections of the previous chapters. A selection of research directions is summarized in the following.

- *Examine and Support Additional Collaboration Requirements*

  The use case studies illustrate heterogeneity of the collaboration requirements in different collaboration scenarios. Research in future work could examine the applicability of the service composition for additional requirements, e.g., in additional use case studies. For example, collaborative creation of slide sets or source code demand support for document models with non-hierarchical structures. In addition, collaboratively created presentations or multi-media documents involve temporal oder behavioral models which could be integrated into the collaboration model. Additional investigations include the application of the presented solution to different workgroup structures, from hierarchical with a central leader to peer-to-peer, the development and assessment of additional communication channels as well as the integration of real-time sensor data through adapters.

  Communication is a common coordination mechanism during collaboration especially in open, community-driven document creation like in pattern repositories [69]. Future work should therefore examine the integration of classical communication mechanisms in the presented collaboration model, e.g., synchronous discussion in chats, or annotation and comments. Version control and traceability can be considered a coordination mechanism. Future work could therefore examine a version control mechanism suitable for evolving compositions of services including suitable UIs. Besides the extension of the collaboration model as regards coordination mechanisms for concurrency control, the set of participation protocols could be extended with additional social communication protocols like negotiation or notification. During collaborations, different collaboration mechanisms might be used in different phases [13]. Future research could investigate if and how seamless transitions between different collaboration mechanisms can be supported by the presented solution.

- *Optimize Coordination Rule Mechanism*

  Besides optimization of the component or composition models, e.g., through supporting additional collaboration mechanisms as described above, the rule model demands
  optimization in two respects. First, the definition and management of coordination
  rules might be too complex for participants. Examining and ensuring usability for
  ECA rules, especially the management of interdependent rules, is an open research
  topic in general. As a first step, common rules required or applied during collaboration could be examined, e.g., in additional use case studies. These rules might then be
  reused and configured by collaboration participants, e.g., leveraging a dialog UI.

  Second, implicit relationships between rules might exist which might result in conflicts
  or undesired side effects. For example, different execution orders of rules might result
  in different states of results or contributions. A first step towards addressing this issue is
  the identification of general as well as collaboration model specific potential conflicts.
  As outlined in Section 5.3, existing approaches like static analysis or prioritization of
  rules could then be applied or adapted.

- *Evaluate Use Case Studies in Field*

  The empirical evaluation of the presented or additional use case studies in order to
  evaluate their usability and suitability appears to be a logical next step. Results of empirical studies might be used to improve the collaboration model in general, or examine
  if humans are able to understand and handle evolving documents including dynamic
  contents. Evaluation of CSCW systems, however, is difficult as the reproduction of
  social, economical, organizational, and motivational aspects and influences of collaboration in a lab situation is almost impossible [54]. Evaluation of such systems is a
  research area on its own. Research as regards this thesis towards these goals could
  be the application of selected collaboration model features in different collaboration
  scenarios in order to evaluate and improve their usability, e.g., the ability to create
  adapters, events or rules.

- *Refine Framework for Collaboration Applications*

  As described in Section 7.3, the collaboration model and infrastructure provide a set of
  components which can be used and tailored by collaboration system providers. In this
  respect, the collaboration model resembles frameworks in software engineering which
  optimally provide reusable software components while supporting suitable adaptation
  to specific application requirements [33]. The focus of the research described in this
  thesis is the examination of the applicability of service composition for different scenarios of collaborative document creation, rather than the design of a framework. Fu-

ture work, therefore, includes the examination of usability and suitability of the collaboration model as framework, e.g., through evaluating design decisions by instantiation of additional collaboration use case studies. Additional use case studies might help in identifying and refining required components and hot spots of the framework.

- *Address Legal, Privacy, and Security Questions*

  In order to collaborate, members of different organizations might apply collaboration systems on the Web or in the Cloud offered by independent, third party providers. A number of legal as well as privacy and security issues exist during collaborative creation of documents on the Web. Assuming that the presented collaboration infrastructure is offered as a service on the Web, these issues need to be addressed in order to enable trust in and increase benefit of the presented solution for inter-organizational collaboration. The collaboration model enables a new kind of dynamic, composed documents which is not considered by current law. For example, during collaborative creation of offerings, humans add parts to documents created by others which requires clarification of liabilities, e.g., in case of illegal document contents.

  Collaboration systems on the Web frequently realize multi-tenancy and isolate data of different tenants, i.e., organizations. Collaborating persons from different organizations, however, might want to use and share specific data of one tenant. Collaboration systems, e.g., a Cloud-enabled implementation of the collaboration model, should therefore ensure that particular data can be exchanged whereas other data stays isolated. In addition, collaboration system providers should secure the system such that even the provider can not access data, e.g., in order to create activity logs. Existing solutions like encryption, anonymization, or role and access right models need to be adapted to usable privacy and security mechanisms with good performance for novel distributed systems on the Web.

To conclude, this thesis presents a novel solution for coordinating service compositions in support of collaborative document creation. The solution supports the flexible composition and coordination of activities and contents contributed by human and non-human providers into collaboratively created documents. The presented collaboration model is a promising approach for the development of collaboration systems which balance flexibility and coordination as required in many cases of human collaboration. Open research directions, however, show that further challenges need to be tackled in order to advance the presented results to usable, practicable, and accepted solutions, potentially leading to a new understanding of flexible collaboration support and dynamic documents.

Bibliography

[1] "cooperation". Oxford Dictionaries. April 2010. Oxford University Press. http://oxforddictionaries.com/definition/cooperation (accessed April 16th, 2012).

[2] W. v. d. Aalst, M. Dumas, and A. H. M. t. Hofstede. Web Service Composition Languages: Old Wine in New Bottles? In *Proceedings of the 29th Conference on EUROMICRO*, EUROMICRO '03, pages 298–305, Washington, DC, USA, 2003. IEEE Computer Society.

[3] W. v. d. Aalst, A. H. M. T. Hofstede, and M. Weske. Business Process Management: A Survey. In *Proceedings of the 2003 International Conference on Business Process Management*, BPM'03, pages 1–12, Berlin, Heidelberg, 2003. Springer-Verlag.

[4] W. v. d. Aalst, M. Weske, and D. Grünbauer. Case handling: a new paradigm for business process support. *Data & Knowledge Engineering*, 53(2):129–162, 2005.

[5] M. Adams, A. ter Hofstede, D. Edmond, and W. v. d. Aalst. Worklets: A Service-Oriented Implementation of Dynamic Flexibility in Workflows. In *On the Move to Meaningful Internet Systems 2006: CoopIS, DOA, GADA, and ODBASE*, volume 4275 of *Lecture Notes in Computer Science*, pages 291–308. Springer, 2006.

[6] R. Alarcon, E. Wilde, and J. Bellido. Hypermedia-Driven RESTful Service Composition. In *Proceedings of the 2010 International Conference on Service-oriented Computing*, ICSOC'10, pages 111–120, Berlin, Heidelberg, 2011. Springer-Verlag.

[7] G. Alonso, F. Casati, H. A. Kuno, and V. Machiraju. *Web Services - Concepts, Architectures and Applications*. Data-Centric Systems and Applications. Springer, 2004.

[8] M. A. Babar and I. Gorton. A Tool for Managing Software Architecture Knowledge. In *Proceedings of the Second Workshop on SHAring and Reusing Architectural Knowledge Architecture, Rationale, and Design Intent*, SHARK-ADI '07, Washington, DC, USA, 2007. IEEE Computer Society.

[9] N. Baloian, F. Claude, R. Konow, and S. Kreft. E-Breaker: Flexible, Distributed Environment for Collaborative Authoring. In *Proceedings of the 2009 13th International Conference on Computer Supported Cooperative Work in Design*, CSCWD '09, pages 173–178, Washington, DC, USA, 2009. IEEE Computer Society.

[10] J. Becker, K. Bergener, and M. Voigt. Supporting Creative Group Processes - Groupware for Communication and Coordination. In *AMCIS 2010 Proceedings. Paper 94*, 2010.

[11] J. Becker, M. Matzner, and O. Müller. Comparing Architectural Styles for Service-Oriented Architectures – a REST vs. SOAP Case Study. In *Information Systems Development*, pages 207–215. Springer US, 2010.

[12] C. Beierle and G. Kern-Isberner. *Methoden wissensbasierter Systeme: Grundlagen, Algorithmen, Anwendungen*. Computational Intelligence. Vieweg+Teubner Verlag, 2008.

[13] A. Bernstein. How Can Cooperative Work Tools Support Dynamic Group Process? Bridging The Specificity Frontier. In *Proceedings of the 2000 ACM Conference on Computer Supported Cooperative Work*, CSCW '00, pages 279–288, New York, NY, USA, 2000. ACM.

[14] R. P. Biuk-Aghai. *Patterns of Virtual Collaboration*. PhD thesis, University of Technology, Sydney, 2004.

[15] S. Boll, W. Klas, and U. Westermann. Multimedia Document Models: Sealed Fate or Setting Out for New Shores? *Multimedia Tools and Applications*, 11(3):267–279, 2000.

[16] P. Bottoni and R. Genzone. A Resource-Based Framework for Interactive Composition of Multimedia Documents. In *Proceedings of the 3rd ACM SIGCHI Symposium on Engineering Interactive Computing Systems*, EICS '11, pages 271–276, New York, NY, USA, 2011. ACM.

[17] J. M. Boyer, C. F. Wiecha, and R. P. Akolkar. A REST Protocol and Composite Format for Interactive Web Documents. In *Proceedings of the 9th ACM Symposium on Document Engineering*, DocEng '09, pages 139–148, New York, NY, USA, 2009. ACM.

[18] J. Brønsted, K. M. Hansen, and M. Ingstrup. Service Composition Issues in Pervasive Computing. *IEEE Pervasive Computing*, 9(1):62–70, 2010.

[19] R. Bruns and J. Dunkel. *Event-Driven Architecture: Softwarearchitektur für ereignisgesteuerte Geschäftsprozesse*. Springer, 2010.

[20] M. K. Buckland. What is a "Document"? *Journal of the American Society for Information Science*, 48(9):804–809, 1997.

[21] D. C. A. Bulterman and L. Hardman. Structured Multimedia Authoring. *ACM Transactions on Multimedia Computing, Communications, and Applications (TOMCCAP)*, 1(1):89–109, 2005.

[22] T. Burkhart and P. Loos. Flexible Business Processes-Evaluation of Current Approaches. *Proceedings of Multikonferenz Wirtschaftsinformatik MKWI 2010*, pages 1217–1228, 2010.

[23] F. Casati, S. Castano, and M. Fugini. Managing Workflow Authorization Constraints through Active Database Technology. *Information Systems Frontiers*, 3(3):319–338, Sept. 2001.

[24] F. Casati, F. Giunchiglia, and M. Marchese. Liquid Publications: Scientific Publications meet the Web. Technical Report DIT-07-073, Dep. of Information and Communication Technology, University of Trento, Italy, December 2007.

[25] F. Casati and M.-C. Shan. Dynamic and adaptive composition of e-services. *Information Systems*, 26(3):143–163, 2001.

[26] S. Ceri, F. Daniel, M. Matera, and A. Raffio. Providing flexible process support to project-centered learning. *IEEE Transactions on Knowledge and Data Engineering*, 21(6):894–909, 2009.

[27] D. Chakraborty and A. Joshi. Dynamic Service Composition: State-of-the-Art and Research Directions. Technical Report TR-CS-01-19, Dep. of Computer Science and Electrical Engineering, University of Maryland, Baltimore, USA, December 2001.

[28] K. Crowston. A Taxonomy of Organizational Dependencies and Coordination Mechanisms. Working paper series, MIT Center for Coordination Science, 1994.

[29] F. Daniel, M. Imran, S. Soi, A. De Angeli, C. R. Wilkinson, F. Casati, and M. Marchese. Developing Mashup Tools for End-Users: On the Importance of the Application Domain. *International Journal of Next-Generation Computing*, 3(2), 2012.

[30] F. Daniel and G. Pozzi. An Open ECA Server for Active Applications. *Journal of Database Management (JDM)*, 19(4), 2008.

[31] U. Dayal, M. Hsu, and R. Ladin. Business Process Coordination: State of the Art, Trends, and Open Issues. In *Proceedings of the 27th Very Large Databases Conference (VLDB 2001)*, pages 3–13, 2001.

[32] A. De Lucia, F. Fasano, G. Scanniello, and G. Tortora. Enhancing collaborative synchronous UML modelling with fine-grained versioning of software artefacts. *Journal of Visual Languages and Computing*, 18(5):492–503, 2007.

[33] S. Demeyer, T. D. Meijler, O. Nierstrasz, and P. Steyaert. Design Guidelines for "Tailorable" Frameworks. *Communications of the ACM*, 40(10):60–64, 1997.

[34] N. Desai, P. Mazzoleni, and S. Tai. Service Communities: A Structuring Mechanism for Service-Oriented Business Ecosystems. In *Digital EcoSystems and Technologies Conference, 2007. DEST '07. Inaugural IEEE-IES*, pages 122–127, February 2007.

[35] C. Dorn, R. N. Taylor, and S. Dustdar. Flexible Social Workflows: Collaborations as Human Architecture. *IEEE Internet Computing*, 16(2):72–77, 2012.

[36] P. Dourish, W. K. Edwards, J. Howell, A. LaMarca, J. Lamping, K. Petersen, M. Salisbury, D. Terry, and J. Thornton. A Programming Model for Active Documents. In *Proceedings of the 13th annual ACM Symposium on User Interface Software and Technology*, UIST '00, pages 41–50, New York, NY, USA, 2000. ACM.

[37] S. Draxler and G. Stevens. Supporting the Collaborative Appropriation of an Open Software Ecosystem. *Computer Supported Cooperative Work*, 20(4-5):403–448, 2011.

[38] S. Dustdar. Caramba – A Process-Aware Collaboration System Supporting Ad hoc and Collaborative Processes in Virtual Teams. *Distributed and Parallel Databases*, pages 45–66, 2004.

[39] S. Dustdar and K. Bhattacharya. The Social Compute Unit. *IEEE Internet Computing*, 15(3):64–69, May 2011.

[40] S. Dustdar, D. Schall, F. Skopik, L. Juszczyk, and H. Psaier. *Socially Enhanced Services Computing: Modern Models and Algorithms for Distributed Systems*. Springer, 2011.

[41] S. Dustdar and W. Schreiner. A Survey on Web Services Composition. *International Journal of Web and Grid Services*, 1(1):1–30, 2005.

[42] S. Dustdar and H. Truong. Virtualizing Software and Humans for Elastic Processes in Multiple Clouds – a Service Management Perspective. *International Journal of Next-Generation Computing*, 3(2):109–126, 2012.

[43] M. Eckert. *Complex Event Processing with XChangeEQ*. PhD thesis, Ludwig-Maximilians-Universität München, December 2008.

[44] C. A. Ellis, S. J. Gibbs, and G. Rein. Groupware: Some Issues and Experiences. *Communications of the ACM*, 34:39–58, January 1991.

[45] A. Espinosa, J. Lerch, and R. Kraut. Explicit vs. Implicit Coordination Mechanisms and Task Dependencies: One Size Does Not Fit All. In *Team cognition: Understanding the factors that drive process and performance*, pages 107–129. American Psychological Association, 2004.

[46] Z. Fiala, M. Hinz, K. Meissner, and F. Wehner. A Component-Based Approach for Adaptive Dynamic Web Documents. *Journal of Web Engineering*, 2(1):58–73, 2003.

[47] R. T. Fielding. *Architectural Styles and the Design of Network-based Software Architectures*. PhD thesis, University of California, Irvine, 2000.

[48] P. Frederiks and T. van der Weide. Information modeling: The process and the required competencies of its participants. *Data & Knowledge Engineering*, 58(1):4–20, 2006.

[49] E. Gamma, R. Helm, R. Johnson, and J. Vlissides. *Design Patterns: Elements of Reusable Object-Oriented Software*. Addison-Wesley Longman Publishing Co., Inc., Boston, MA, USA, 1995.

[50] L. Gao, S. D. Urban, and J. Ramachandran. A Survey of Transactional Issues for Web Service Composition and Recovery. *International Journal of Web and Grid Services*, 7(4):331–356, 2011.

[51] A. Gerlicher. Computer-Supported Cooperative Work (CSCW) – kollaborative Systeme und Anwendungen. In *Kompendium Medieninformatik*, X.media.press, pages 143–195. Springer Berlin Heidelberg, 2007.

[52] R. J. Glushko and T. McGrath. *Document Engineering: Analyzing and Designing Documents for Business Informatics and Web Services*. MIT Press, Cambridge, Mass, 2005.

[53] E. M. Goncalves da Silva, L. Ferreira Pires, and M. J. van Sinderen. Dynamic Composition of Services: Why, Where and How. In *Proceedings of the Second International Workshop on Enterprise Systems and Technology (I-WEST 2008), Enschede, The Netherlands*, pages 73–85, Portugal, May 2008. INSTICC Press.

[54] J. Grudin. Groupware and Social Dynamics: Eight Challenges for Developers. *Communications of the ACM*, 37(1):92–105, 1994.

[55] A. Hartman, A. N. Jain, J. Ramanathan, A. Ramfos, W.-J. Van der Heuvel, C. Zirpins, S. Tai, Y. Charalabidis, A. Pasic, T. Johannessen, and T. Grønsund. Participatory Design of Public Sector Services. In *Proceedings of the First International Conference on Electronic Government and the Information Systems Perspective*, EGOVIS'10, pages 219–233, Berlin, Heidelberg, 2010. Springer-Verlag.

[56] M. Hertzum. Six Roles of Documents in Professionals' Work. In *Proceedings of the Sixth European Conference on Computer Supported Cooperative Work*, pages 41–60, Norwell, MA, USA, 1999. Kluwer Academic Publishers.

[57] A. R. Hevner, S. T. March, J. Park, and S. Ram. Design Science in Information Systems Research. *MIS Quarterly*, 28(1):75–105, 2004.

[58] S. Holmlid. Participative, co-operative, emancipatory: From participatory design to service design. *1st Nordic Conference on Service Design and Service*, 2009.

[59] V. Hoyer, K. Stanoesvka-Slabeva, T. Janner, and C. Schroth. Enterprise Mashups: Design Principles towards the Long Tail of User Needs. In *Proceedings of the 2008 IEEE International Conference on Services Computing - Volume 2*, SCC '08, pages 601–602, Washington, DC, USA, 2008. IEEE Computer Society.

[60] R. Hull. Artifact-Centric Business Process Models: Brief Survey of Research Results and Challenges. In *On the Move to Meaningful Internet Systems: OTM 2008*, volume 5332 of *Lecture Notes in Computer Science*, pages 1152–1163, Berlin, Heidelberg, 2008. Springer-Verlag.

[61] ISO/IEC. ISO/IEC 14977:1996(E). Information technology – Syntactic metalanguage – Extended BNF. Online. http://standards.iso.org/ittf/PubliclyAvailableStandards/s026153_ISO_IEC_14977_1996(E).zip (accessed January 12th, 2013), 1996.

[62] M. Janssen and R. Feenstra. Socio-Technical Design of Service Compositions: A Coordination View. In *Proceedings of the 2nd International Conference on Theory and Practice of Electronic Governance*, ICEGOV '08, pages 323–330, New York, NY, USA, 2008. ACM.

[63] J.-Y. Jung, J. Park, S.-K. Han, and K. Lee. An ECA-based framework for decentralized coordination of ubiquitous web services. *Information and Software Technology*, 49(11-12):1141–1161, 2007.

[64] M. Kapuruge, J. Han, and A. Colman. Support for Business Process Flexibility in Service Compositions: An Evaluative Survey. In *Proceedings of the 2010 21st Australian Software Engineering Conference*, ASWEC '10, pages 97–106, Washington, DC, USA, 2010. IEEE Computer Society.

[65] D. Karastoyanova, A. Houspanossian, M. Cilia, F. Leymann, and A. Buchmann. Extending BPEL for Run Time Adaptability. In *Proceedings of the Ninth IEEE International EDOC Enterprise Computing Conference*, EDOC '05, pages 15–26, Washington, DC, USA, 2005. IEEE Computer Society.

[66] J. Katz and B. R. Martin. What is research collaboration? *Research policy*, 26(1):1–18, 1997.

[67] R. Kern, C. Zirpins, and S. Agarwal. Managing Quality of Human-Based eServices. In *Service-Oriented Computing — ICSOC 2008 Workshops*, pages 304–309, Berlin, Heidelberg, 2009. Springer-Verlag.

[68] R. Khalaf and F. Leymann. On Web Services Aggregation. In *Technologies for E-Services*, volume 2819 of *Lecture Notes in Computer Science*, pages 1–13. Springer Berlin / Heidelberg, 2003.

[69] A. Kittur and R. E. Kraut. Beyond Wikipedia: Coordination and Conflict in Online Production Groups. In *Proceedings of the 2010 ACM Conference on Computer Supported Cooperative Work*, CSCW '10, pages 215–224, New York, NY, USA, 2010. ACM.

[70] M. Klein. Coordination Science: Challenges and Directions. In *Coordination Technology for Collaborative Applications*, volume 1364 of *Lecture Notes in Computer Science*, pages 161–176, London, UK, 1998. Springer-Verlag.

[71] M. Koch. *Unterstützung kooperativer Dokumentenbearbeitung in Weitverkehrsnetzen*. PhD thesis, München, Techn. Univ., 1997.

[72] O. Kopp, B. Wetzstein, R. Mietzner, S. Pottinger, D. Karastoyanova, and F. Leymann. A Model-Driven Approach to Implementing Coordination Protocols in BPEL. In *Business Process Management Workshops*, volume 17 of *Lecture Notes in Business Information Processing*, pages 188–199. Springer Berlin Heidelberg, 2009.

[73] S. Kumaran, R. Liu, P. Dhoolia, T. Heath, P. Nandi, and F. Pinel. A RESTful Architecture for Service-Oriented Business Process Execution. In *Proceedings of the 2008 IEEE International Conference on e-Business Engineering*, pages 197–204, Washington, DC, USA, 2008. IEEE Computer Society.

[74] K. Kuutti. Activity theory as a potential framework for human-computer interaction research. *Context and consciousness: Activity theory and human-computer interaction*, pages 17–44, 1996.

[75] A. Lamarca, W. K. Edwards, P. Dourish, J. Lamping, I. Smith, and J. Thornton. Taking the Work out of Workflow: Mechanisms for Document-Centered Collaboration. *Proceedings of the Sixth European Conference on Computer Supported Cooperative Work (ECSCW'99)*, (September):12–16, 1999.

[76] M. D. P. Leland, R. S. Fish, and R. E. Kraut. Collaborative Document Production Using Quilt. In *Proceedings of the 1988 ACM Conference on Computer-Supported Cooperative Work*, CSCW '88, pages 206–215, New York, NY, USA, 1988. ACM.

[77] D. M. Levy. Document Reuse and Document Systems. *Electronic Publishing*, 6(4):339–348, 1993.

[78] V. Liptchinsky, R. Khazankin, H.-L. Truong, and S. Dustdar. Statelets: Coordination of Social Collaboration Processes. In *Proceedings of the 14th International Conference on Coordination Models and Languages*, COORDINATION'12, pages 1–16, Berlin, Heidelberg, 2012. Springer-Verlag.

[79] J. Long. *ITIL Version 3 at a Glance: Information Quick Reference*. Springer Publishing Company, Incorporated, 1st edition, 2008.

[80] P. B. Lowry, A. Curtis, and M. R. Lowry. Building a Taxonomy and Nomenclature of Collaborative Writing to Improve Interdisciplinary Research and Practice. *Journal of Business Communication*, 41(1):66–99, 2004.

[81] R. Lu and S. Sadiq. A Survey of Comparative Business Process Modeling Approaches. In *Proceedings of the 10th International Conference on Business Information Systems*, BIS'07, pages 82–94, Berlin, Heidelberg, 2007. Springer-Verlag.

[82] D. Luckham and W. R. Schulte. Event Processing Glossary – Version 2.0. Event Processing Technical Society, July 2011.

[83] N. Lundberg and T. I. Sandahl. What do artifacts mean to us in work. *Proceedings of the 22nd Information Systems Research Seminar in Scandinavia*, pages 363–372, 1999.

[84] T. Malone and K. Crowston. The Interdisciplinary Study of Coordination. *ACM Computing Surveys (CSUR)*, 26(1):87–119, 1994.

[85] T. W. Malone, K.-Y. Lai, and C. Fry. Experiments with Oval: A Radically Tailorable Tool for Cooperative Work. *Transactions on Information Systems (TOIS)*, 13(2):177–205, 1995.

[86] J. E. McGrath. Time, Interaction, and Performance (TIP) : A Theory of Groups. *Small Group Research*, 22(2):147–174, May 1991.

[87] G. Monsieur. *Pattern-based coordination in process-based service compositions*. PhD thesis, Katholieke Universiteit Leuven, 2010.

[88] A. Mørch. *Computers and design in context*, chapter Three Levels of End-User Tailoring: Customization, Integration, and Extension, pages 51–76. MIT Press, Cambridge, MA, USA, 1997.

[89] H. Motahari-Nezhad, C. Bartolini, S. Graupner, S. Singhal, and S. Spence. IT Support Conversation Manager: A Conversation-Centered Approach and Tool for Managing Best Practice IT Processes. In *Proceedings of the 2010 14th IEEE International Enterprise Distributed Object Computing Conference (EDOC '10)*, pages 247 –256, October 2010.

[90] S. Noël and J.-M. Robert. Empirical Study on Collaborative Writing: What Do Co-authors Do, Use, and Like? *Computer Supported Cooperative Work*, 13(1):63–89, 2004.

[91] A. Norta, M. Hendrix, and P. Grefen. A Pattern-Knowledge Base Supported Establishment of Inter-organizational Business Processes. In *On the Move to Meaningful Internet Systems 2006: OTM 2006 Workshops*, volume 4277 of *Lecture Notes in Computer Science*, pages 834–843. Springer Berlin Heidelberg, 2006.

[92] J. F. Nunamaker, Jr., M. Chen, and T. D. M. Purdin. Systems Development in Information Systems Research. *Journal of Management Information Systems*, 7(3):89–106, 1990.

[93] OASIS. UDDI Spec Technical Committee Draft Version 3.0.2. Online. http://uddi.org/pubs/uddi-v3.0.2-20041019.htm (accessed January 15th, 2013), 2004.

[94] OASIS. Web Services Atomic Transaction (WS-AtomicTransaction) Version 1.1. Online. http://docs.oasis-open.org/ws-tx/wstx-wsat-1.1-spec/wstx-wsat-1.1-spec.html (accessed August 31st, 2012), 2007.

[95] OASIS. Web Services Business Process Execution Language Version 2.0. Online. http://docs.oasis-open.org/wsbpel/2.0/wsbpel-v2.0.html (accessed July 03rd, 2012), 2007.

[96] OASIS. Web Services Coordination (WS-Coordination) Version 1.1. Online. http://docs.oasis-open.org/ws-tx/wstx-wscoor-1.1-spec/wstx-wscoor-1.1-spec.html (accessed July 4th, 2012), 2007.

[97] OASIS. Web Services for Remote Portlets Specification v2.0. Online. http://docs.oasis-open.org/wsrp/v2/wsrp-2.0-spec-os-01.html (accessed October 03rd, 2012), 2008.

[98] OASIS. Web Services Business Activity (WS-BusinessActivity) Version 1.2. Online. http://docs.oasis-open.org/ws-tx/wstx-wsba-1.2-spec.html (accessed August 31st, 2012), 2009.

[99] OASIS. Web Services – Human Task (WS-HumanTask) Specification Version 1.1. Online. http://docs.oasis-open.org/bpel4people/ws-humantask-1.1.html (accessed July 03rd, 2012), 2010.

[100] OASIS. WS-BPEL Extension for People (BPEL4People) Specification Version 1.1. Online. http://docs.oasis-open.org/bpel4people/bpel4people-1.1.html (accessed October 01st, 2012), 2010.

[101] B. Olsen, N. Lund, and G. Hartvigsen. Leaving twentieth-century understanding of documents – From book to eBook to digital ecosystem. In *4th IEEE International Conference on Digital Ecosystems and Technologies (DEST)*, pages 600 –605, April 2010.

[102] OMG. Business Process Model and Notation (BPMN) Version 2.0. Online. http://www.omg.org/spec/BPMN/2.0/ (accessed September 28th, 2012), January 2011.

[103] M. Papazoglou. Service-Oriented Computing: Concepts, Characteristics and Directions. In *Proceedings of the Fourth International Conference on Web Information Systems Engineering (WISE 2003).*, pages 3 – 12, December 2003.

[104] R. Parasuraman and V. Riley. Humans and Automation: Use, Misuse, Disuse, Abuse. *Human Factors: The Journal of the Human Factors and Ergonomics Society*, 39(2):230–253, 1997.

[105] R. Parasuraman, T. B. Sheridan, and C. D. Wickens. A Model for Types and Levels of Human Interaction with Automation. *IEEE Transactions on Systems, Man, and Cybernetics, Part A: Systems and Humans*, 30(3):286–297, May 2000.

[106] N. W. Paton and O. Díaz. Active Database Systems. *ACM Computing Surveys (CSUR)*, 31(1):63–103, 1999.

[107] C. Pautasso. Composing RESTful Services with JOpera. In *Proceedings of the 8th International Conference on Software Composition*, SC '09, pages 142–159, Berlin, Heidelberg, 2009. Springer-Verlag.

[108] C. Pautasso, O. Zimmermann, and F. Leymann. RESTfulWeb Services vs. "Big" Web Services: Making the Right Architectural Decision. In *Proceedings of the 17th International Conference on World Wide Web*, WWW '08, pages 805–814, New York, NY, USA, 2008. ACM.

[109] K. Peffers, T. Tuunanen, M. Rothenberger, and S. Chatterjee. A Design Science Research Methodology for Information Systems Research. *Journal of Management Information Systems*, 24(3):45–77, 2007.

[110] I. Posner and R. Baecker. How People Write Together. In *Proceedings of the Hawaii International Conference On System Sciences*, volume 25, pages 127–127. IEEE Institute Of Electrical And Electronics, 1992.

[111] A. Powell, G. Piccoli, and B. Ives. Virtual Teams: A Review of Current Literature and Directions for Future Research. *SIGMIS Database*, 35(1):6–36, 2004.

[112] R. Power, D. Scott, and N. Bouayad-Agha. Document Structure. *Computational Linguistics*, 29(2):211–260, 2003.

[113] W. Pree. *Design Patterns for Object-Oriented Software Development*. ACM Press/Addison-Wesley Publishing Co., New York, NY, USA, 1995.

[114] A. B. Raposo, L. P. Magalhães, I. L. M. Ricarte, and H. Fuks. Coordination of Collaborative Activities: A Framework for the Definition of Tasks Interdependencies. In *Proceedings of the Seventh International Workshop on Groupware*, CRIWG '01, pages 170–180, Washington, DC, USA, 2001. IEEE Computer Society.

[115] M. Renger, G. L. Kolfschoten, and G.-J. Vreede. Challenges in Collaborative Modeling: A Literature Review. In *Advances in Enterprise Engineering I*, volume 10 of *Lecture Notes in Business Information Processing*, pages 61–77. Springer Berlin Heidelberg, 2008.

[116] L. Richardson and S. Ruby. *RESTful Web Services*. O'Reilly, first edition, 2007.

[117] F. Rosenberg, F. Curbera, M. J. Duftler, and R. Khalaf. Composing RESTful Services and Collaborative Workflows: A Lightweight Approach. *IEEE Internet Computing*, 12:24–31, September 2008.

[118] S. W. Sadiq, M. E. Orlowska, and W. Sadiq. Specification and Validation of Process Constraints for Flexible Workflows. *Information Systems*, 30:349–378, 2005.

[119] D. Schall. *Human Interactions in Mixed Systems - Architecture, Protocols, and Algorithms*. PhD Thesis in Computer Science, Information Systems Institute – Vienna University of Technology (TU Wien), 2009.

[120] D. Schall. A human-centric runtime framework for mixed service-oriented systems. *Distributed and Parallel Databases*, 29(5-6):333–360, 2011.

[121] D. Schall, H.-L. Truong, and S. Dustdar. Unifying Human and Software Services in Web-Scale Collaborations. *Internet Computing, IEEE*, 12(3):62 –68, May-June 2008.

[122] L. Schamber. What Is a Document? Rethinking the Concept in Uneasy Times. *Journal of the American Society for Information Science*, 47(9):669–671, 1996.

[123] K. Schmidt and C. Simone. Coordination Mechanisms: Towards a Conceptual Foundation of CSCW Systems Design. *Computer Supported Cooperative Work*, 5(2-3):155–200, 1996.

[124] U. Scholten, R. Fischer, and C. Zirpins. The Dynamic Network Notation: Harnessing Network Effects in PaaS-Ecosystems. In *Proceedings of the Fourth Annual Workshop on Simplifying Complex Networks for Practitioners*, SIMPLEX '12, pages 25–30, New York, NY, USA, 2012. ACM.

[125] U. Scholten, N. Schuster, and S. Tai. A Pattern Language and Repository for Service Network Management. In *Proceedings of the 2012 IEEE International Conference on Service-Oriented Computing and Applications*, SOCA '12, pages 1–9, Washington, DC, USA, 2012. IEEE Computer Society.

[126] N. Schuster, R. Stein, and C. Zirpins. A Mashup Tool for Collaborative Engineering of Service-Oriented Enterprise Documents. In *Information Systems Evolution*, volume 72 of *Lecture Notes in Business Information Processing*, chapter 12, pages 166–173. Springer Berlin Heidelberg, Berlin, Heidelberg, 2011.

[127] N. Schuster, R. Stein, C. Zirpins, and S. Tai. A Service Mashup Tool for Open Document Collaboration. In *Service-Oriented Computing*, volume 6470 of *Lecture Notes in Computer Science*, pages 713–714. Springer Berlin / Heidelberg, 2010.

[128] N. Schuster, C. Zirpins, and U. Scholten. How to Balance Flexibility and Coordination? Service-oriented Model and Architecture for Document-based Collaboration on the Web. In *Proceedings of the 2011 IEEE International Conference on Service-Oriented Computing and Applications*, SOCA '11, pages 1–9, Washington, DC, USA, 2011. IEEE Computer Society.

[129] N. Schuster, C. Zirpins, S. Tai, S. Battle, and N. Heuer. A Service-Oriented Approach to Document-Centric Situational Collaboration Processes. In *Enabling Technologies: Infrastructures for Collaborative Enterprises (WETICE '09)*, pages 221–226. IEEE Computer Society, 2009.

[130] B. Sengupta, A. Jain, K. Bhattacharya, H.-L. Truong, and S. Dustdar. Who Do You Call? Problem Resolution through Social Compute Units. In *Proceedings of the 2012 International Conference on Service-oriented Computing*, ICSOC'12, pages 48–62, Berlin, Heidelberg, 2012. Springer-Verlag.

[131] M. Shaw. Architectural Requirements for Computing with Coalitions of Resources. *Position paper for First Working IFIP Conference on Software Architecture*, 1999.

[132] E. Silva, J. Martínez López, L. Ferreira Pires, and M. S. van. Defining and Prototyping a Life-cycle for Dynamic Service Composition. In *Architectures, Concepts and Technologies for Service Oriented Computing*, pages 79–90, Portugal, July 2008. INSTICC Press.

[133] D. H. Sonnenwald. Communication roles that support collaboration during the design process. *Design Studies*, 17(3):277 – 301, 1996.

[134] M. Stefik, D. G. Bobrow, G. Foster, S. Lanning, and D. Tatar. WYSIWIS Revised: Early Experiences with Multiuser Interfaces. *ACM Transactions on Information Systems (TOIS)*, 5(2):147–167, 1987.

[135] S. Tai, R. Khalaf, and T. Mikalsen. Composition of coordinated web services. In *Proceedings of the 5th ACM/IFIP/USENIX International Conference on Middleware*, Middleware '04, pages 294–310, New York, NY, USA, 2004. Springer-Verlag New York, Inc.

[136] H. Tellioglu. About Representational Artifacts and Their Role in Engineering. In *Phenomenology, Organizational Politics and IT Design: The Social Study of Information Systems*, pages 1–31. IGI Global, 2012.

[137] M. ter Beek, A. Bucchiarone, and S. Gnesi. Web service composition approaches: From industrial standards to formal methods. In *Proceedings of the Second International Conference on Internet and Web Applications and Services*, ICIW '07, pages 15–, Washington, DC, USA, 2007. IEEE Computer Society.

[138] G. H. ter Hofte and H. J. van der Lugt. CoCoDoc: a framework for collaborative compound document editing based on OpenDoc and CORBA. In *Proceedings of the IFIP/IEEE International Conference on Open Distributed Processing and Distributed Platforms*, ICODP/ICDP '97, pages 15–33, London, UK, UK, 1997. Chapman & Hall, Ltd.

[139] M. Treiber, D. Schall, S. Dustdar, and C. Scherling. Tweetflows: Flexible Workflows with Twitter. In *Proceedings of the 3rd International Workshop on Principles of Engineering Service-Oriented Systems*, PESOS '11, pages 1–7, New York, NY, USA, 2011. ACM.

[140] H.-L. Truong, S. Dustdar, and K. Bhattacharya. Programming Hybrid Services in the Cloud. In *Proceedings of the 10th International Conference on Service-Oriented Computing*, ICSOC'12, pages 96–110, Berlin, Heidelberg, 2012. Springer-Verlag.

[141] S. Vinoski. REST Eye for the SOA Guy. *IEEE Internet Computing*, 11(1):82–84, 2007.

[142] S. Vinoski. Serendipitous Reuse. *IEEE Internet Computing*, 12(1):84–87, 2008.

[143] W3C. SOAP Version 1.2. Online. http://www.w3.org/TR/soap12-part1/ (accessed June 17th, 2012).

[144] W3C. Web Services Description Language (WSDL). Online. http://www.w3.org/2002/ws/desc/ (accessed June 17th, 2012).

[145] B. Weber, M. Reichert, and S. Rinderle-Ma. Change patterns and change support features - enhancing flexibility in process-aware information systems. *Data & Knowledge Engineering*, 66(3):438 – 466, 2008.

[146] S. Weerawarana, F. Curbera, F. Leymann, T. Storey, and D. F. Ferguson. *Web Services Platform Architecture: SOAP, WSDL, WS-Policy, WS-Addressing, WS-BPEL, WS-Reliable Messaging and More*. Prentice Hall PTR, Upper Saddle River, NJ, USA, 2005.

[147] J. Whitehead. Collaboration in software engineering: A roadmap. In *2007 Future of Software Engineering*, FOSE '07, pages 214–225, Washington, DC, USA, 2007. IEEE Computer Society.

[148] R. Wieringa. Design Science as Nested Problem Solving. In *Proceedings of the 4th International Conference on Design Science Research in Information Systems and Technology*, DESRIST '09, pages 8:1–8:12, New York, NY, USA, 2009. ACM.

[149] E. Wittern, N. Schuster, J. Kuhlenkamp, and S. Tai. Participatory Service Design through Composed and Coordinated Service Feature Models. In *Proceedings of the 10th International Conference on Service-Oriented Computing*, ICSOC'12, pages 158–172, Berlin, Heidelberg, 2012. Springer-Verlag.

[150] E. Wittern and C. Zirpins. On the Use of Feature Models for Service Design: The Case of Value Representation. In *Towards a Service-Based Internet. ServiceWave 2010 Workshops*, volume 6569 of *Lecture Notes in Computer Science*, pages 110–118, Berlin, Heidelberg, 2011. Springer Berlin / Heidelberg.

[151] X. Xu, L. Zhu, Y. Liu, and M. Staples. Resource-Oriented Architecture for Business Processes. In *Proceedings of the 2008 15th Asia-Pacific Software Engineering Conference*, APSEC '08, pages 395–402, Washington, DC, USA, 2008. IEEE Computer Society.

[152] J. Yang and M. P. Papazoglou. Service components for managing the life-cycle of service compositions. *Information Systems*, 29(2):97–125, 2004.

[153] J. Yu, B. Benatallah, F. Casati, and F. Daniel. Understanding mashup development. *IEEE Internet Computing*, 12:44–52, September 2008.

[154] O. Zimmermann. *An Architectural Decision Modeling Framework for Service-Oriented Architecture Design*. PhD thesis, Institut für Architektur von Anwendungssystemen der Universität Stuttgart, Germany, 2009.

[155] O. Zimmermann, J. Koehler, F. Leymann, R. Polley, and N. Schuster. Managing Architectural Decision Models with Dependency Relations, Integrity Constraints, and Production Rules. *Journal of Systems and Software*, 82(8):1249–1267, 2009.

[156] M. zur Muehlen, J. V. Nickerson, and K. D. Swenson. Developing web services choreography standards: the case of REST vs. SOAP. *Decision Support Systems*, 40(1):9–29, 2005.

List of Abbreviations

API	application programming interface
BPEL4People	WS-BPEL Extension for People
BPMN	Business Process Model and Notation
CEP	complex event processing
CRUD	create, read, update, and delete
CSCW	computer-supported cooperative work
DYNO	Dynamic Network Notation
EBNF	Extended Backus-Naur Form
ECA	event-condition-action
EMF	Eclipse Modeling Framework
EPL	Event Processing Language
GUI	graphical user interface
HATEOAS	Hypermedia as the Engine of Application State
HCI	human-computer interaction
HPS	human-provided services
HTTP	Hypertext Transfer Protocol
ITIL	Information Technology Infrastructure Library
PPR	Portland Pattern Repository
REST	Representational State Transfer
S3	Amazon Simple Storage Service
SCU	Social Compute Unit
SFM	service feature model
SOA	service-oriented architecture
SOC	service-oriented computing
UDDI	Universal Description Discovery & Integration
UI	user interface
UML	Unified Modeling Language
URI	Uniform Resource Identifier
WS-BPEL	Web Services Business Process Execution Language
WSDL	Web Services Description Language
WSRP	Web Services for Remote Portlets
WYSIWIS	What You See Is What I See

List of Figures

List of Tables

Index